Love to a Whore's Daughter

Life and faith through the lens of grace and redemption

LISA F. BARNES

Cover and layout design by
Adriana Rivera

Love to a Whore's Daughter
Life and faith through the lens of grace and redemption
Lisa F. Barnes
2015 Frontier Press

Cover and layout design by
Adriana Rivera

Barnes, Lisa F.
Love to a Whore's Daughter

October 2015

ISBN 978-0-9968473-0-8

Printed in the United States on recycled paper

To Anthony, my handsome best friend.
You are God's greatest gift to me.
You love me just as I am, while encouraging me to be
the best version of myself I could be.
You are a man of integrity, love, and compassion
and the best father to our beautiful beige babies.

Thanks also for being my external filter.

Good looking out, Boo.

ACKNOWLEDGEMENTS

Majors Kevin and Linda Jackson: Thanks for encouraging this project, believing in me, and spurring me on.

Lt. Colonels Joe and Shawn Posillico: You have loved and supported me for years. I am more thankful for you than I have words to express.

Lorrie Davis, Joesphine Morton, Jen Arens- My Big Three: You have each cared for me during dark days, and shared the light of Jesus when I thought all hope was lost. Thanks for loving me when you had every reason not to.

Commissioners Jim and Carolyn Knaggs: Your visionary leadership rocks, and your compassion for the one lost sheep is evident in all you do.

To our camp staff: You have blessed my heart and done amazing things for the kingdom by showing Jesus and loving the lost. Heaven is surely more crowded because of you.

TABLE OF CONTENTS

Foreword... ix

Introduction: Let's Rock.. xi

More than a Food Box.. 1

Misunderstanding Forgiveness............................... 5

You Don't Matter.. 9

God-Sized Dreams.. 13

My Biggest Mistake.. 17

This Mask is Heavy... 21

I am Woman; Hear Me ... Do Whatever I Wanna Do........ 25

"I Don't Care if the World Knows What My Secrets Are"....... 29

Wounds... 33

Create... 37

A Drunken Lie... 41

Color 45

Tattoo Evangelism.. 49

Comparison That Kills.. 53

Judge Me.. 57

Wild Things and Unloveables................................. 61

The Christian Cage... 67

A Love Letter to the Life Changers......................... 71

The Family We Choose.. 75

Serving with Jerks.. 79

The Dating Test... 85

Love and Sex Are Not Synonyms............................ 89

Crushing Expectations.. 93

Foot-Phobic.. 97

Nobody's Puppet... 103

Season of Terror.. 107

The Fight... 111

The Curse of Coasting on Good Enough........................... 115

Exploding Pedestals.. 119

Conclusion.. 123

FOREWORD

Lisa is a voice of vulnerability and courage, strength and compassion. The sincerity of her heart is tattooed on her body—it is real, visible and unhidden for the world to see.

With refreshing honesty and brutal sincerity, Lisa brings us her story—how she has shifted her identify as a daughter of a prostitute to a daughter loved by God.

Lisa's story captures the intricacies of life. From once feeling unwanted and discarded, she walks us through her journey of finding forgiveness and acceptance, joy and belonging. She shares lessons learned on overcoming the abuse of neglect and the pain of rejection, to embracing the joy of ministry and the beauty of community.

It is her incredibly poignant testimony that has shaped her vocation today. As a pastor in The Salvation Army, she has been a light to so many who have similarly experienced abuse. Yet her message is not only a narrative of redemption for women in abuse, but for all who have experienced woundedness.

To us—the pastor, prostitute, spiritual leader, and addict—she says, "Lay the mask down."

Lisa developed practices of faith that have helped to bring about her own healing. Her example encourages us to share our stories, our deepest and darkest secrets, acknowledging that healing is nurtured in community. There, as we embrace our weaknesses and failures, we find the courage to be human. The mask is slowly lifted and we are able to recognize our true identity in Christ.

In this honest confessional, we recognize there is hope of redemption.

We live in a world where prostitution runs rampant, orphans are perpetually abused, and hurting children are unseen. In this book, Lisa captures these stories of reality that we may prefer not to hear. Because if we listen, we know that we will be compelled to respond to our own need for healing, compelled to act in compassionate justice on behalf of others, and compelled to hold together the hands of the broken.

As I heard such stories around the world—compelling me to work in restoring dignity with survivors of sexual violence in Kenya and Zambia— I am further compelled by Lisa's story. I am compelled to recognize the areas of brokenness in my own life and within my own backyard. Our neighbors, our classmates, our families and our friends are the unseen—they are the forgotten, abandoned and abused former Lisas in our community. Like Lisa, we must lay our own mask down to reach out our hands and raise each other up.

Walking us through her personal journey toward healing, Lisa holds our hand in the process—reminding us that in the pain, in the abuse, in the darkness and woundedness of our world, our redeeming God of Grace is ever present.

—Nikole Lim
Co-founder and International Director of *Freely in Hope*.

INTRODUCTION

Let's Rock

In Joshua 4, the nation of Israel crossed the Jordan River and Joshua told one dude from each tribe to grab a rock from the riverbed. They made a pile of these regular, everyday rocks to serve as a memorial to a time when God intervened on behalf of his people. God saw them through a crazy tough time, and he wanted the kids, teens, young adults, and all the generations that were to come to know how amazing he is, and that he was and is living and active in their lives.

God could have done this very differently. God could have told the people to make a beautiful statue to remember what he'd done. He chose just to use rocks. Rocks are common. Rocks aren't beautiful. Rocks are rough and not always easy to work with. Rocks are just rocks. But God uses ordinary things to show his grace and presence all the time. God works with hard rocks and hard heads. For that I am thankful.

God could have also told the people that he wanted them to put the rocks in the center of the city so everyone could see them all the time. But God asked his people to put the rocks (in verse five) in the middle of the Jordan River. In the middle. That means that for the most part, these stones would be hidden by the water—that is, until times of drought when the waters receded.

Drought back in the day in the Middle East was the worst of the worst. It brought panic and death and despair. God wanted to offer a reminder of his presence, his love, his care, and his intervention when his people would need it the most, when times seemed the darkest and they felt crippled by hopelessness.

This book is about life and faith and all the messy bits in between. This book exposes the piles of stones that God put in my life to show his faithfulness. Some of my stone piles will be different than yours; others may be the same. My hope is that, by reading this book, you will recognize the piles of stones around you when you are in the pits. You will know that you are not defined by times of fear, or shame, or abandonment, or hurt, or wounds, or secrets, or even joys and accomplishments. You are a child of God, no matter what.

There are questions for reflection at the end of each chapter. These can be just for you, but asking the hard questions with a buddy may lead to more honesty and accountability. (I recommend that, but I'm not the boss of you, so you do what you want.)

I hope you enjoy this read. It's my heart. It's my story. I'm looking forward to rejoicing in God's faithfulness with you as we journey together.

God rocks.

More than a Food Box

There was a knock at the door. That always made me nervous. Was it an addict looking for his next hit? Was it my mom's drug supplier looking for the money she owed him? Was it a john expecting my mother to finish what she started? Was it the cops? Was it child protective services? Usually a knock at the door brought fear and bad news. Today the knock meant something very different. I answered and there was a woman I'd never seen before. She was older, and when she smiled she had the deepest wrinkles that have ever existed in the history of wrinkles. Maybe that was just my perspective. Most people don't live so long in the projects. (Too many hazards in the hood. Not enough apple eaters or marathon runners.)

Her name was Grandma Gene. She wasn't my grandma. I don't even know if she was anyone's grandma. But I learned later that's what everyone called her. In her arms was a box. In its former life, this box held bananas. I remember the Chiquita symbol on the side, and the soggy corner where the writing was brown and distorted. I stuck my thirteen-year-old head inside and I saw more food in that one box than we'd had in our kitchen in weeks: boxes, cans, a little produce, and a small chicken.

When Grandma Gene brought that box to our home, I can only assume what she was thinking: *I know this woman, Margaret. When she comes to us for help she's often strung out. She has a girl with her who always looks so scared. Last time I saw Margaret she looked too sick to come to The Salvation Army to pick up a food box herself. Maybe I will just drop one off on my way home. Maybe Margaret will see that Jesus loves her, and maybe that little girl will see it too.*

If that is what Grandma Gene was thinking, she wasn't wrong. But there was a lot more flooding my mind at the time. Things like, *This means I won't have to steal food for a few days. Maybe my mom will stay home tonight instead of turning tricks until the sun comes up. Is this what normal kids feel like, not consumed with the thoughts of fighting to eat?*

My mom came up behind me and invited our visitor into the trash heap we called home. Grandma Gene went into our kitchen to set the box down. There she saw a part of my life I struggled hard to keep secret. My mother, aside from being an addict, drug dealer, and prostitute, was a hoarder. Our kitchen was covered in garbage. The sink was filled with moldy dishes. The counters were littered with trash, cigarette butts, empty bottles of booze, and all manner of disgusting things. I was so embarrassed. Grandma Gene knew. She saw into my trapped, chaotic existence. At

1

that moment, it was like she saw into the deepest part of who I was and came face to face with my fear and sadness. She turned to me and, instead of looking at me with pity or disgust like I was anticipating, she smiled a little and said, "Let's put this in the living room for now." It was like she didn't even notice the filth. All she saw was a girl and her sick mother who needed help and compassion.

Grandma Gene set the box down on one of the only accessible surfaces in our home. My mother offered her a seat, which was kind of a joke because there was no seat, aside from the lopsided off-brand Lazy Boy she was sitting on, and she was clearly not giving it up for Grandma Gene. There was a small stained loveseat, but the stains didn't matter; it was piled two-feet-high with newspapers from the past few years. Grandma Gene told my mom she would love to sit and chat, and immediately started moving some of the newspapers so she had a small corner of the dirty couch to occupy.

Grandma Gene and my mother sat and talked for nearly half an hour. I sat on the floor watching in amazement. I felt like I was in a parallel universe. No one EVER sat and talked with my mom without expecting anything in return. Some people made small talk before asking for drugs or sex, but they never just sat and talked. She looked at my mom in the eye, genuinely laughed at her jokes, and treated her like she was a human. This was something I'd never seen. She continued to ignore the mess, the floor-to-ceiling fog of cigarette smoke, and my mother's foul mouth. (My mom was very creative with her use of curse words. I think that might be where I get it from—my creativity that is, not so much the foul mouth.)

The conversation ended and as I walked Grandma Gene to the door (more in an effort to clear her path than to be polite—my gracious manners came later in life), she stopped and asked me if I would like to come to youth group. She said they met every week and had a lot of fun together. I thought for a minute. I didn't have any friends, didn't know how to act in social situations, and was always afraid of people knowing who I really was or where I came from. But something about this invitation was different. It had to be because Grandma Gene was different. I told her that I would like to come to youth group. Just before the door shut, she said, "Great! The van will be here to pick you up tomorrow at five."

With that one encounter, my life was forever altered, both in the immediate and in the long-term. Grandma Gene gave us much more than a food box that day. She gave us dignity. Never did she treat us like we were a lesser form of humanity, which is what I felt like every moment of my life. She gave us a few days of freedom from the bondage of the projects. We didn't have to steal to eat, and my mom didn't have to turn tricks. She made me think that there was a chance that life could be different.

She invited me to be a part of something bigger than my prison of poverty and self-loathing. I went to youth group the next day. Then the next week. Then I went multiple times a week. At first I was so afraid that people would find out what my life was really like. They did find out, but nothing changed. They treated me just like Grandma Gene had. I wasn't the poor, sad, destructive daughter of a drug dealer and whore. For the first time in my life, I was just Lisa. I was valuable and loved. I was taught that my life could be what I chose it to be, not what my community in the hood told me it had to be.

I am overwhelmed with gratitude for Grandma Gene and the day she dropped off a food box and changed my life. She has since gone to be with the Lord. When I kick the bucket, one of the things I'm looking forward to most is hanging out with Grandma Gene and Jesus, talking story and laughing with her like she laughed with my mom. I bet her wrinkles will be long gone, along with the ghost of the girl I used to be.

Grandma Gene's visit was my introduction to what The Salvation Army is and what it stands for. It changes lives by redeeming and restoring those who are at the margins of society, especially the young ones caught in the crossfire of their parents' choices. Even now, almost twenty years later, this is the lens through which I view our movement. Everything we do should center on Jesus and the redemption he brings, which works out pretty well, because that's how I want to operate generally in life. That principle is the foundation of this book. How does the redemption and restoration we find in Jesus translate into everyday aspects of our lives? Where does Jesus stand when a Christian has a random hook-up, or when someone is struggling with doubt and lack of faith?

In no way am I claiming to have all of the answers to the pressing questions of the millennial generation. But the questions need to be asked and the conversations need to be had. Thanks for joining me, just a girl from the hood who knows what it's like to feel lost and abandoned, who has had her fair share of doubt and questions, and who is looking to Jesus for the answers to the messy bits of life.

Questions for Reflection:

- Has there been a time in your life when someone offered you dignity instead
- of judgment or condemnation?
  What can we do as a church to walk alongside people who live in the margins?
- Is there a Lisa in your life?
- Search for Scriptures that speak to helping the hopeless or those in poverty.

Misunderstanding Forgiveness

I forgive you. Three of the most powerful words we can share with each other. Those words have the ability to change hearts, alter circumstances, and restore the most broken of things. "I love you" gets a lot of hype, but it is often overused. In my case, I love my husband and my kids ... and chocolate, and nail polish, and Internet videos of cats playing with babies. When I say I love these things, there is no sarcasm in my tone. I really do love them, especially chocolate. (I think chocolate is evidence that God is real and he loves me.)

When we say we love things, we don't put any extra thought or consideration into those words. But if I were to tell you that I forgive nail polish—even when it smudges or gets bits of potato chips stuck in the top coat—I would sound like a crazy person, or like I didn't really understand what forgiveness was. (P.S., I also love potato chips. Sometimes when I'm ready for some Doritos, I eat them before the polish is dry and mess up at least half of my digits. Don't judge me.) But when we sincerely forgive someone, it causes people to stop in their tracks. We don't forgive as often as we could. When you take out the Jesus element of forgiveness, it is even more difficult to find.

It is important to forgive. It is freeing to forgive. It is liberating to forgive. And it is humbling to be forgiven. But before we can become people who freely forgive, it would be beneficial for us to know what forgiveness is, and what it isn't.

So in looking up Scriptures on forgiveness, I stumbled on one of the most hardcore of passages, *"For if you forgive men when they sin against you, your heavenly Father will also forgive you. But* [here comes the hardcore part] *if you do not forgive men their sins, your Father will not forgive your sins"* (Matt. 6:14-15 NIV). Yikes!

Important point of context: these verses are found right after Jesus tells us how to pray with the Lord's Prayer. I think Jesus knew that when he talked about prayer and forgiving others, he needed to include an explanation of how big a deal this really is. If it's a big deal to him, it should be a big deal to us, too.

I think that authentic forgiveness doesn't really have anything to do with the person we are forgiving. Most of the time, the person doesn't know, or maybe even doesn't care. We forgive for ourselves. We forgive so we can let it go and feel whole. Maybe Jesus commands us to forgive truly and completely so we can see a small glimpse of how he forgives us. If we are capable of doing this, then most definitely the creator of the universe is capable of forgiving us when we come to the cross and repent of our junk.

As we journey towards being forgiving folks, let's take a look at some forgiveness impostors. These are the things out there that try to trick us into thinking that they are elements of forgiveness. Sometimes they are a part of the process, but sometimes they just aren't.

Excuses. Everyone has them, and they all smell. Making an excuse for someone who has done you dirty or deeply hurt you is not forgiveness. Dismissing what someone has done—maybe saying it wasn't really a big deal or you didn't take it personally—is not the same as forgiving what has happened. This burns bridges and adds layers to the masks we wear.

Forgiveness is not for wimps. If the act of forgiveness seems quick or easy, there is a good chance that it isn't really forgiveness at all. Authentic forgiveness demands effort from the one doing the forgiving. Yeah, it gets easier over time, with practice, and as we grow as followers of Jesus. But most of the time, it's not easy, and it's not disguised as a bag of excuses.

They don't have to be sorry for us to forgive them. Folks who hurt us may never see what they did as wrong, or even be aware of how it affected us. There are even a few people out there, I refer to them as super-jerks, who know that we are hurt or that they did something that they shouldn't have, and they are in no way remorseful for any of it. Praise the Lord that there is forgiveness even for them.

Our forgiveness isn't dependent upon the other person feeling bad, or even admitting wrongdoing. Because forgiveness is for us, and is not really even about the offending party, how the other person feels about the situation is inconsequential to us offering legit forgiveness and moving on.

Denial and passive acceptance are not forgiveness. Sometimes it's easier to ignore what happened and just stay silent about it all. Not confronting an offense or injustice doesn't mean that we have forgiven the jerk who did it.

There are people who freak out at the thought of confrontation. They think if they keep silent to maintain peace, then they are doing what's right. But there is no peace in their hearts. They harbor the hurt and keep all of the negativity bottled up. That's not beneficial for anyone. Like I said before, forgiveness isn't easy. Sometimes we have to do what is difficult to achieve real peace and have the relationships we want. That means there are times when we've gotta have the courage to confront, for healing's sake.

Maybe if I claim the entire problem, it will just go away. Forgiveness also isn't blaming ourselves for everything. There are times when we've had a part to play in the drama that went down, but saying it's all our fault all the time doesn't have anything to do with forgiveness. Even if our bad choices make us major players in the problem, forgiveness can still happen. These kinds of situations may take a little more grace and acceptance of our own roles.

Reconciled relationships are not always required. Sometimes people hurt us in a way that makes a fully reconciled relationship with them a bad idea. If we can tell by their lack of remorse that there is a good chance they aren't going to stop doing the hurtful thing, then maybe they should just kick rocks.

For example, I think of people who have been abused physically. We would in no way encourage a victim of molestation to be in any kind of relationship with the person who caused such hurt. This also applies to people who have no remorse for the rude way they choose to talk to you, or for insults they slam in your direction. Sometimes the best thing for us to do is to forgive the jerks (then stop referring to them as jerks), and pray for them as we allow them to exit stage left out of our lives.

Out of all of the forgiveness imposters listed above, I can relate the most to not needing a reconciled relationship. This is where I am with my birth mother. I've shared a bit about her, and the vices that crippled her life. I wish I could say that the Lord moved in a mighty way and she now sings in the church choir, or plays first chair cornet. At this point she is in her early sixties, still caught up in her addiction and—mind-bogglingly—still running the streets.

Growing up with her was rough to say the least, and I could make a list of her offenses that could make even the meanest of super-jerks cringe. If anyone has a get-out-of-forgiveness-free card, I do. But that Scripture verse from Matthew 6 lets us know that no one has a get-out-of-forgiveness card.

I lived with my birth mother until I was fifteen. Not consistently; there were about thirty-five different foster and group homes that were sprinkled in throughout that time. Most were during third and fourth grade. (Please don't ask me to multiply or divide. I have no idea how. When most kids are learning those things, I was bouncing from place to place, hoping for a safe landing somewhere.)

Through all my years with my mom, I remember actively hating her—even as early as kindergarten. I moved in with my corps officers (pastors) when I was fifteen. They granted me asylum from the penitentiary that was my life, and it was because they removed me from such a crazy environment that I am not on the same trajectory that I was once on. Them and Jesus, of course.

So I lived with them for about three years, hating my birth mother the whole time. I worked at camp and led kids to the Lord while hating my mother. I met and married my husband while hating my mother. Then I became a mother, and terror shook me. I was scared that I was going to do everything wrong because I had a crack head for my main example, and was even more afraid that my child was going to hate me like I hated my mother.

Something had to give ... but it didn't. I kept up my resentment and anger until I was a second year cadet in Salvation Army seminary school, preparing myself to love and serve the lost, while still being totally okay with hating my mother. Then the thought of being a hypocrite, standing behind the pulpit and preaching a message of love and forgiveness while being content in my discontent, was enough for me to face that demon.

I couldn't do it on my own. I needed help to talk about all the things she had done and put me through. I saw a counselor every week, and she helped me work through my mommy issues. I learned to legit forgive my mom and others who had hurt me. At this point, I am confident in saying that I have true and complete forgiveness toward my mother. In the same breath, I am just as secure in saying that we will never have a reconciled relationship.

Caveat: this isn't my prescription for everyone, and it isn't really the best solution. It would be better for us to be able to communicate, or have any kind of interaction at all. However, she is still a hurtful and abusive person. She is destructive and horribly racist, among other things. As a wife to my handsome black husband and a mother to my beautiful beige babies, it is my duty to protect them, even if that means keeping my mom as far away from them as possible. I pray for her. I am thankful that she released me to the care of others. And I hope that one day she truly finds the Lord.

My forgiveness for her freed me from a tormented past. It guides my steps as a confident mother now (both to the children who have lived in my abdomen and the hundreds of children and young adults I've met in ministry who live in my heart). I know that I'm not her and her mistakes aren't mine. I am thankful for the freedom that comes with forgiveness and the peace of knowing what forgiveness isn't.

Questions for Reflection:

- What is holding you back from forgiving those who have hurt you?
- What have you done to offend or hurt others that you need to seek forgiveness for?
- Does Scripture ever give us an "out" for forgiveness?
- How will things be different for you if you actively pursue forgiveness?

Note: My list of forgiveness imposters was inspired by: *Psychology, Theology, and Spirituality in Christian Counseling*, by Mark R. McMinn, Ph.D.

You Don't Matter

What's your mantra? You know, something you say repeatedly, or something that helps you to remember important things. Mantras are originally a Buddhist thing, but don't let that freak you out. We use this concept as Christians, but don't always have a name for it. Maybe yours is a phrase or verse you use when you are meditating on God's Word.

I have a few. My good Christian example is from my life verse. This became my life verse while I was in the last group home I ever lived in. I was fifteen. My mom and I had been fighting all day. I came home from school and it was World War III in my apartment.

A few days before this all went down, we agreed I could invite some friends over to stay the night. It was my first sophomore year in high school. (Yes, by first I do mean that there was a second sophomore year. Do your homework kids; it *really* is important.) Never ever had anyone sleep over at my house, nor had I slept over at anyone else's. For most of my childhood, I didn't think that sleepovers were even a real thing. I thought it was something that the perfect white families did on TV, like eating dinner together and having dads.

Things were starting to look up for my mom and me. She was only strung out a few days a week as opposed to every day. I was going to church and, in an attempt to live out what I was taught there, I was being more respectful and not dropping the f-bomb as regularly. So I asked my mom if we would be able to have a couple of my friends stay the night. When I got home from school, she was strung out and the house was a hot mess. We started fighting, and things got real. There was hair pulling and face punching on both sides. At about 11 p.m., she went to the front of the apartment and threw my backpack out the door. She looked at me and told me to get out.

I walked to the corner store and called 911. I told the dispatch lady what had happened and she sent a squad car to pick me up. The cop put me in the back of the car and went to talk to my mom. After a few minutes, he went to the trunk for a camera and walked back to my apartment. He took pictures and talked to my mom some more. When he was finished, he sat in the driver's seat, motionless and silent.

After what felt like an eternity of silence that was so deafening my ears were ringing, I asked what happened. "If you were a dog, we wouldn't let you go back in there," he told me with sadness in his voice.

"Yeah, it's pretty bad, huh?" I replied. Then more time passed in silence, with neither of us moving in the dark squad car. In the pit of my emptiness I found enough courage to ask, "What did she say?"

I thought he didn't hear me, until I heard him sniffle and his voice crack as he replied, "She said that she doesn't want you anymore. She said that you are too much trouble."

I wish I could say that I was surprised or sad about these words, but this was my life. She said those kinds of things to me all the time. When she didn't use her words to convey those messages, she used her actions.

He took me to a girls-only group home. All I had with me were the clothes I was wearing and my backpack. Thankfully, that day I had taken my Bible to school, so it was still in my backpack. I still have that Bible. It is a *God's Word Translation* paperback in a fuzzy pink Bible case. It is still one of my most treasured possessions.

Late the first night I was reading Romans, and I got to chapter five. Verses three and four stopped me in my tracks. They say: *But that's not all. We also brag when we are suffering. We know that suffering creates endurance, endurance creates character, and character creates confidence* (GW). These words aren't easy to understand and live out for normal people, and they seemed impossible for a girl who had just been thrown away by the only family member that she'd ever known.

Rejoice in my sufferings? Instead of making me angry or confused like some hardcore passages do, these words gave me instant comfort. It was like the Lord said to me, "Lisa, this is for you, right now, in the middle of this hurt and struggle. Rejoice. I love you and I will never throw you away. Rejoice. Things will get better."

That chunk of Scripture is my mantra—different parts of it for different things. Like while I was struggling to finish high school, when there was so much I didn't know and I was behind in what seemed like every way possible, I would say to myself over and over, "Endurance. Character. Confidence. Endurance. Character. Confidence." It helped me get through. I didn't excel. I slid through on the mercy of teachers who knew my past and saw that there might be potential in me for something greater.

Change happens and our lives shift. Sometimes those shifts make us feel like our hearts are being cut out with a dull blade. In those times I've said over and over, "Suffering creates endurance. Suffering creates endurance." It is amazing what a few words can do to keep our focus on what matters and settle the most anxious of hearts.

I'm a fan of the mantra.

That was my good Christian example of a mantra. Another phrase that is a regular utterance of my heart is, "You don't matter."

be first" thing. When we accept Jesus as the Lord of our lives and give up who we are for the cause of Christ, we have to give up our selfish spirit. If we don't, things will always feel unbalanced.

I've been married for over ten years. I know what you're thinking: *Lisa, you are so young and beautiful! How is it that you have been married for that long?* Well, thank you for your compliments. I recognize them as truth and you as a kind soul.

The main reason my husband and I aren't at each other's throats all the time is what we call "the big piece of chicken rule." (We are chubby kids, so most of my illustrations and analogies have to do with food.) The big piece of chicken rule means we always give each other the best of what is available. At dinner, whoever is serving will give the other the biggest piece of chicken, or the last slice of pizza. When our main concern is to put others first, and make sure they have everything they need, we are not concerned with ourselves. The "What about me?" thoughts never come into play. We aren't fighting about feeling left out or ignored. We don't matter.

Selfishness destroys when given the opportunity. Living the mantra "you don't matter" irradiates that disease from our lives.

If I'm being totally honest, I use the "you don't matter" mantra in other ways. When someone is acting like a dirt bag, I may or may not say internally, "You don't matter." If I feel like someone is devaluing things that are important to me, or even who I am as a person, I say to myself, "You don't matter," not to be mean-spirited, but to reassure myself who really matters (the Lord), who defines me (still the Lord), and the one I am most accountable to (you guessed it, the Lord for the hat trick!).

We get into self-doubt and generally get off track when we let the opinions of those who don't really matter take up too much of our brain space. People matter, but their opinions ... not always. That may mean that we need to let our people-pleasing desires, or our pride, go. But that's okay, because it's not about you. You don't matter. It's only about Jesus.

This takes all kinds of wisdom to figure out. Because sometimes, people are coming to you with things that may kinda sting, but are justified. If you are doing something wrong or out of vain ambition and you are lucky enough to have a true friend call you out on your crap, that does matter. My continuous prayer is that I would see the opinions of others for what they really are, and make changes as necessary—or smile and nod as I walk away from those who are just trying to cut me down.

You (meaning YOU, the one reading this) don't matter. We have given up ourselves for the cause of Christ. If you are fighting to be number one, you will fail and fall. You don't matter. You can't come first. You can't push people aside to get your way then wonder why God isn't blessing your efforts. If you have shoved him off the throne to make sure you get the best seat in the house, then things are likely to suck.

Mantras. They help get us through, if paired with wisdom.

Questions for Reflection:

- What are some mantras you've used in the past to help get you through the tough times?
- Search the Scriptures for possible mantras for the future. Commit them to memory.
- Have you given the opinions of others too much weight in your life? Are there hurtful words that have become truth that you need to let go of?
- What are some tangible things you can do to put others first?

God-Sized Dreams

Who are you? What do you want to do for the Lord? We are all very different people, and we all have work to do. But that doesn't mean that we all need to do the same stuff. And praise God for that.

A big part of knowing what kind of service we would thrive in is knowing who we are. I'm now a fan of spiritual gift inventories. I haven't always been a fan. They kind of remind me of the quizzes I used to take from *Seventeen* magazine, like "What kind of girlfriend are you?" but Christian style.

The last time I took one of these, it told me that out of the ten or twelve spiritual gifts that were evaluated, my highest was encouragement, and I was pissed. I thought, *What a lame spiritual gift! Some people got much cooler gifts—things like wisdom or faith—and I got encouragement. I have the extra special ability to tell people, "Good job!" I must be highly favored....*

What is cool, though, is that your gifts work together to make a concoction that is you. And with the specific makeup of gifts that you bring to the table, you can do things for Jesus that many others cannot.

My next-in-line gift is discernment, which I think is much cooler than encouragement. My discernment gift helps me to see through people's walls pretty quickly. It is easy for me to tell if someone is being dishonest. I've learned to use this power for good instead of evil. When I was younger and I thought people were lying, I would just call them out in front of everyone and embarrass them. Now I know that people are often dishonest because they are afraid or uneasy about trusting others. This helps me to feel compassion instead of anger or resentment. And that is for sure a gift from the Lord, because in my humanness, I am not a very compassionate individual. (The last gift on my inventory list was mercy.)

With me, when you mix encouragement and discernment, you get an offspring gift. I call it the spiritual gift of being-able-to-make-people-cry. So if I am in a conversation, often I am able to see deeper into a people's hearts, to see where their hurts are, and God gives me the words of encouragement that they need to hear right at that point.

When I'm in these kinds of conversations and the other people involved start crying and they get embarrassed, I stop them and tell them not to worry—that their tears are my fault and I just do that to people; it's my spiritual gift. Most of the time, they think I am kidding. I am not.

What I used to think was the lamest spiritual gift has become my clear place in the body of Christ. There are many things I don't do well. But the more I embrace what I can do, and take every opportunity to use that for the kingdom, the more I am able to see positive changes in the direction of Jesus.

So who are you? What are your gifts and abilities? What are your passions? What are your dreams? And, do your dreams scare you? They should freak you out. If our dreams don't scare us, then we probably aren't dreaming big enough. We have the creator of the universe in our corner. Why would we limit the impact we could have because we are afraid or stuck on our puny dreams?

Don't get me wrong, the little things matter. The things we do everyday in our local congregations and communities totally matter. But could there be more?

In Acts 1:8, Jesus says these last words before he is taken up, *"But you will receive power when the Holy Spirit comes on you; and you will be my witnesses in Jerusalem, and in Judea and Samaria, and to the ends of the earth"* (NIV). Jesus was a smart dude, and his words often mean more than what we, in our world today, are able to understand. This verse is a great example of that.

The people Jesus is talking to in Acts are from Jerusalem. This was kind of like the disciples' home base. They were familiar with this place, the people were familiar with them, and it wasn't a difficult place for them to be.

Jesus wanted them to be witnesses for him in their home base. He wanted them to live lives where he was glorified and spoken about regularly. This wouldn't be a terribly difficult request. It would be like me saying to you, "Hey, when you go to work and school, it would be cool if you loved your friends and invited them to church. It would also be a neat thing if you volunteered at church or led something." We should all be doing those things. Be my witnesses in Jerusalem. Be my witnesses at home.

Numero dos on that list was to be a witness in Judea. This was a little further away from home. The disciples may not have known as many people there, or been as comfortable. It would be like the difference between you crashing on your best friend's couch for the night and crashing on your Aunt Sandra's couch (when you've only met her once, she has a beard and you don't really know what to do with all of that).

They would have had to work harder and be a ton more intentional to do the same kinds of things in Judea as they were doing in Jerusalem. Being a witness in our home base is good, but Jesus asks us for more. What are your dreams for doing more? What could you do for Jesus that maybe makes you a little uncomfortable? What's your plan for working harder and going the extra mile?

Then we are off to Samaria. Dang, Jesus. Samaria? That was the worst place possible for the disciples. It was full of folks who were very different from them, and who desperately needed Jesus. Jesus wants his disciples (even present day disciples) to go and do things that are way difficult. Life for Christ isn't supposed to be comfortable. As we grow in our faith and in our service to the Lord, things should get increasingly more intense.

Our God-sized dreams should have us always moving towards more for him. It's important to finish what you start. It's important to allow things to progress in God's time, and in a way that makes sense. It probably wouldn't be wise for a person to accept Jesus as a personal Savior on a Tuesday and set off on a year-long mission trip on Thursday. God wants us to grow as people and learn to do more for the cause of Christ as we mature in our relationship with Jesus.

Jesus, being Jesus, doesn't even stop with Samaria. He tells us to be witnesses at our home base, then to go a little further out of our comfort zone, then to go to the places that scare us. (Jesus talked in story often. Maybe a scary place for you has more to do with your personal fears than an actual scary physical location.) THEN Jesus tells us to go to the ends of the earth. What does that even mean? Who the heck knows? Jesus does, and I think that is good enough. The ends of the earth are different for all of us.

What are your God-sized dreams? What could you do for the kingdom that scares you to the core?

Right now you are holding my God-sized dream. I like to write. It is a passion the Lord put on my heart. He made it clear that I am to be as honest and vulnerable in this book as I could ever be. I am sharing stories of my soul that I don't often share. Now they are printed words and I can never take them back. The hope is that others will draw closer to the Lord through this book somehow. Even just one. Full disclosure: I am terrified. My God-sized dream involves risk and fear.

When people come to the ends of their lives, rarely do they say that they wish they had watched more TV, or played more video games, or talked to their kids less, or attempted fewer of their dreams or desires. People don't wish they had played it safe. Risk and fear are a part of faith and ministry; they are not your enemy or feelings that you should run from.

Do things no one else has ever done, and do things that people have told you are out of your reach. Do them! And once they're done, remind people that the Lord uses the least of the least of these to accomplish great things for his glory.

Go to the ends of the earth with your God-sized dreams and do the unimaginable for Jesus.

Questions for Reflection:

- What are your spiritual gifts? Take an inventory if you haven't already. You might be surprised.
- What would you do for Jesus if there were nothing holding you back?
- Make a list of local things you can do for the kingdom. Start small—but start something.
- What are you afraid of when it comes to accomplishing your dreams in ministry?
- Find Scriptures about fear or service and put them where you will see them regularly.

My Biggest Mistake

I've made mistakes—a lot of mistakes. If we were to sit together and compare a list of the worst choices we've made, I'm pretty sure I would win, or at least raise your eyebrows and make you reconsider being in the same room with me without a witness present.

Most of my mistakes you will never know, and I am thankful for that. There is one mistake that I am the most ashamed of. In fact, if I could reverse one choice in my life, this is the one I would pick. I hope that we are still friends after I tell you this story.

I had a friend named Jamie. (I am lying. Her name wasn't Jamie. I would be a dirty rat for spilling all the beans and giving you her real name, come on now.) Jamie and I had become great friends in a very short amount of time. It would be fair to say that she was my best friend, and I was hers.

As friends do, we shared parts of our stories that we usually kept hidden. I shared my deepest fears: dark silence and the mystery under the bed. I know it sounds like I'm kidding, but I am truly terrified of the space underneath the bed. I think it is one of those things that most kids are afraid of, but the fear dissolves as we mature. Maybe I'm not mature enough yet. Whatever—it freaks me out.

Jamie shared things with me; some were lighthearted, and some were not. There was one thing that she shared. It was her deepest and darkest. I was the second person she had ever shared this thing with. (No, I'm not gonna tell you what it was. Man, you guys are so nosey!) And rightly so. This was a big thing. This thing scared me. I felt because I loved Jamie, I really needed to share this thing with someone else, because this already big thing could easily become a HUGE thing, and that would have been horrible.

So I found someone we both trusted and loved, and I shared my best friend's deepest, darkest secret. This third party was kind and wanted to help too. So this person—let's call her Sarah (this is also a lie; I just really like the name Sarah)— went to Jamie and asked her about the secret. I don't know what Jamie's response was. My guess is that it was one of anger, or fear, or resentment, or a cocktail of all of these emotions.

Even still, this is not the part of the story that I regret with my whole heart. It's coming....

After the conversation between Jamie and Sarah, Jamie came to me, looked me in the eye, and asked if I had shared the secret. I returned her eyeball-to-eyeball stare, and with confidence in my voice told her, "No. I didn't tell anyone."

That's it, my biggest regret. I had a great friend who trusted me with everything. She trusted me with a secret that she had kept with her for a long time. This secret had held her captive, as secrets tend to do. Telling me about it had the potential to release her from that captivity. To begin healing and growing. But then I ruined it. Not by sharing the secret, because sometimes secrets need to become public to set people free; they can hurt more if allowed to grow and fester in the darkness. But I lied. I looked Jamie in the face—my best friend who had trusted me with so much—and lied.

Have you ever made a mistake, and then your pride jumped into the mix to convince you that it would be a horrible, life-threatening thing for you to admit you were wrong, and that you should do whatever it takes to save face? Yeah, that happened to me too.

Then I acted like I hadn't done anything wrong in any direction. Things escalated, and I hurt Jamie more than I've ever hurt anyone. Even now, I am ashamed of the girl I was. I eventually apologized and moved on after our horrible fall out, probably still clinging to some aspects of my pride and wanting to think it really wasn't that big of a deal.

Until it happened to me.

I have a friend, Mia. (Dang, I am such a liar. I promise that the rest of this book is totally true. But I am lying up a storm in this chapter. I hope you forgive me.) Mia and I also became very close. I shared my super-secret with her. The only time I'd ever shared this before was when I was dating my husband and it was getting serious. This secret is so big that I thought he should know before he made a lifelong commitment to me, because this might be a deal breaker. (And I was terrified of commitment, and I was 80% sure that he would hear this and run for the hills. He didn't, praise the Lord.)

Mia told my secret! Can you believe it? How could someone who was supposed to be my friend do something like this?... Oh wait; this is what it feels like? It was like someone had ripped my heart out. It didn't matter to me what Mia's motivations were, or how much she was justified in sharing my dirties with the person that she did. I trusted her, and she spit on that trust. (That was how it felt in my mind at that time. I do not feel that way anymore.)

My first rational thought, after the blind rage subsided, was: Jamie. This was how she felt. I didn't fully comprehend the emotional impact of what I had done by betraying my friend's trust until it happened to me. Because of what had gone down previously with Jamie and me, I was able to repair things with Mia before it got to that same level.

I received a gift that day—a gift of empathy. I don't ever want to be that friend again. The worst kind of friend is the one who breaks the trust of another. The amazing part of this story is that Jamie eventually forgave me. I repented to her and to the Lord. She is an incredibly gracious woman. I am thankful that she is in my life, and she is an example to me in many ways. But even now, when I see her I still feel a twinge of guilt or shame. I feel nothing, no anger or resentment, when I see Mia. The position of the trust breaker is a far worse place to be in than the one whose trust gets broken.

We need each other. We were designed to live in community. We can't function at optimum performance levels if we aren't journeying with people who can share in our burdens and in our triumphs. The rough part of community is that if we aren't trustworthy, we won't have access. No one will want to share burdens with you if you are infamous for blabbing people's business. Are you the kind of person others go to when they need a listening ear?

Psalm 133:1 says, *How good and pleasant it is when brothers live together in unity!* (NIV). The word for unity is also translated as "togetherness." We gotta do this together. I need you, and you need me. We *could* operate as lone wolves, but why would we want to? What benefit would we gain by living apart from other believers, or by not letting people into our lives? With real talk, you can get burned. Others could do to you what I did to Jamie or what Mia did to me. But growth and laughter and opportunities to be united abound, and the times when people do us dirty are miniscule in comparison.

If the creator of the universe operates in community (Father, Son, Holy Spirit—undivided in essence and co-equal in power and glory), then how crazy is it for us to think that we would be fine if we lived sans community? We need each other.

I need you. Others in your life need you. Let's work together to do kingdom business. Be real with others, even at the risk of being hurt. God is much bigger than any hurt we could experience here. We have work to do. Let's do it together.

I have a couple qualifications. First, choose your closest confidants carefully. Not everyone is ready to know all about you, to know things that you may not want the whole world to know. In time they could be, but while you are journeying with others, use wisdom and discernment as you choose those you will share your super-secrets with. Helpful hint: if they gossip with you about others, there is a high probability that they will gossip with others about you. Make sure you don't fit into this group. It's not fun to be lumped with this bunch.

Second, if a person shares a secret that she has (or might in the future) hurt herself or someone else, you cannot keep this to yourself. Best-case scenario is to tell the friend that this is something that she needs help with. Then go with her as she tells a responsible party about what's going on, maybe a counselor or pastor. Not all secrets need to be kept secret, especially if someone isn't safe.

Questions for Reflection:

- Are you the kind of person who lets people in? Why or why not?
- Do you keep the confidences of others?
- What are some Scripture verses about the value of community?
- Share or journal about a time when someone betrayed your trust. If you are brave enough, maybe even share or journal about a time when you were the one doing the betraying.
- Has the body of Christ ever stood up and carried you through a difficult time, even if it was just one person representing the body?

This Mask is Heavy

I am a mediocre juggler, metaphorically speaking of course. Juggling tangible objects is absolutely out of the question for me. I can hardly play catch effectively, let alone catch and release in repeated succession without dropping the ball or hitting myself in the face. I'm talking about the juggling we do in life, with the different facets of who we are. Aspects of our world that we do all we can to keep separate.

In high school, church Lisa and school Lisa were very different people, and never the two shall meet. It wasn't like I was extraordinarily bad at school and an angel at church. Really, I was pretty bad in both places, but at church I was accepted. At church I didn't have to fake it. At school, my whole life was a lie.

At church it was common knowledge that my mom was a whore and I lived in the projects. Thankfully, they loved and embraced me anyway. I think the whole Jesus thing had a lot to do with that. At school, there was no Jesus motivation to treat me with kindness, and kids are ruthless. So it was beneficial for me to put up the best front I could while I was there.

The mask I wore at school often consisted of me being a big fat bully. Reason number one why my two worlds couldn't mix: What self-respecting bully would invite her victims to church? I had a reputation to maintain, and I would lose all of my intimidation power if I did that. (It's crazy how we think sometimes.)

I did all I could to act like everything in my life was fine. I avoided any conversations about what was going on at home. It was tough to have conversations about parents being unfair or annoying with "normal" kids when you grew up like I did. If friends were complaining about their parents taking away TV privileges for not cleaning their rooms, me jumping in with, "Uh, I know. My mom has been MIA for three days, and figuring out meals with no money is getting irritating," doesn't really work. I wasn't "normal," but keeping up the appearance was a high priority.

Ideally, people should feel comfortable enough to be the same everywhere. At church I was safe; at school I wasn't. I think that if you are going to live separate lives, this is probably the best-case scenario. Church should be where we feel safe and welcome. Where people know what's going on in our lives and love us just the same. When I was at church, I could relax. I could be the Lisa that I really was with no fear that I would be tossed aside or belittled. At church I also had leaders who loved me and the rest of the teens enough to call us on our crap when we needed it.

Unfortunately, I think the opposite is often true—people don't always feel safe at church. When this is the case, you feel like you need to walk on eggshells, remembering who knows what about you, and who you told half-truths to. Questions arise about who you shared what with, and how much did you really tell them? Was there a story you told to keep part of yourself secret, and now you need to remember that story as if it were gospel. That is a lot to carry around, and that mask can quickly become unbearable.

Many stop going. It's just too much. Too much to keep so many plates spinning, especially if you are a part of the group that doesn't feel loved or accepted at church. Why work so hard to perfect these different masks if you don't think that people are going to care about you anyway?

Friends, I challenge you to do something incredibly brave. I challenge you to lay the masks down. Maybe not all at once; that could be a little overwhelming for you *and* for those you are now gonna be real and vulnerable with. But is there one person at your church you can trust enough to show what's really going on?

If the answer to that is no, then what about in your outlying Christian community? Maybe there is someone you worked at camp with, or went to a youth retreat with. Maybe the person doesn't go to your church, or even live in your community, but this is a person you feel you can go to and share your hurts. Those masks get heavy. The longer you struggle to keep them up, the more likely you will be to give up and leave the church. Put them down before they take over everything.

We can only keep up a façade for so long. There is a good chance that people will find out the things we are keeping secret, even if we don't always want them to. Let's say, for example, you are a cutter or are struggling with some other form of self-harm. Would you rather take that secret, that struggle, and go to a trusted person to talk it through and figure out the next steps together, or keep it to yourself, fight that battle alone and afraid? Someone sees the cuts on your arm that you wouldn't have ever chosen to show. Now things are all over the place. People are being told that just shouldn't be, and you are being pulled in a million different directions. Your mask is now controlling you.

I don't know about you, but I don't ever want to be in a place where I feel like I'm spiraling out of control because I wasn't brave enough to take authority back before it was ripped from me. Again, it's important to share with wisdom, because there are dirt bags who will take our masks and secrets and be merciless. But I think there are far less dirt bags than we think, if we just give people a chance rather than assuming that's who they are.

Please don't hear me say that any of this is easy. This may be one of the toughest things that you do. It may feel like you have a lot to lose, and you might. But I can say from personal experience, there is nothing more freeing than knowing you are a welcomed and vulnerable part of the body of Christ. That people really know you, even the messy bits, and they love you just the same.

Colossians 3:9-11 from *The Message* says, *Don't lie to one another. You're done with that old life. It's like a filthy set of ill-fitting clothes you've stripped off and put in the fire. Now you're dressed in a new wardrobe. Every item of your new way of life is custom-made by the Creator, with his label on it. All the old fashions are now obsolete. Words like Jewish and non-Jewish, religious and irreligious, insider and outsider, uncivilized and uncouth, slave and free, mean nothing. From now on everyone is defined by Christ, everyone is included in Christ.*

Lying is hard work. I don't want to lie about who I am or what I've done. I don't want to worry about who knows what, or what stories I need to keep straight. Lying to those in my Christian community is yesterday's business. I don't want to worry about the labels people give, or what they may say behind my back. I lay down the masks that used to define me and now surrender fully to the definition I find in Christ, and the inclusion I find in living with him and in unity and honesty with his people.

The freedom that comes from that is better than any fake identity I might have, and there is no turning back.

Questions for Reflection:

· When have you felt like you have had to be someone you weren't? What made you feel that way?
· Are you still wearing those masks, or have you put them down?
· Make a list of the fears that motivate you to keep those masks on.
· Find a passage of Scripture that talks about freedom in Christ. Share it with a friend who may be struggling with this topic.

I am Woman; Hear Me ...
Do Whatever I Wanna Do

*He told his disciples, "I have been given all authority in heaven and earth. There-
fore go and make disciples in all the nations, baptizing them into the name of the Father and of the Son and of the Holy Spirit, and then teach these new disciples to obey
all the commands I have given you; and be sure of this—that I am with you always,
even to the end of the world"* (Matt. 28:18-20 TLB).

I'm a disciple of Jesus. Follower. Believer. Devotee. Learner. And a woman. The
great commission specifically tells us disciples (no gender excluded) to go and
make more disciples in the name of Jesus, inviting them to be a part of the body
of Christ.

There are people (quite a few) who think that in the eyes of God, women have a
lesser status than men do. (I know this sounds crazy, but it's true.)

I am a woman preacher. I am a woman pastor.

I am trained and ordained to bring the Word of God and to show Jesus to those
within my sphere of influence. This bothers people. I am thankful to be a part of a
movement in The Salvation Army that is more egalitarian than most.

Egalitarian: [ih-gal-i-tair-ee-uhn] "the Christian egalitarian view holds that
the Bible teaches the fundamental equality of women and men of all racial and
ethnic mixes, all economic classes, and all age groups, based on the teachings and
example of Jesus Christ and the overarching principles of Scripture" (definition
courtesy of Wikipedia, the free encyclopedia, helping people win arguments
since 2001).

There are several passages of Scripture that show that Jesus wants to empower
women just as much as men to do great things for the kingdom. I am going to challenge you to find some when you've finished this chapter.

My most favorite passage that shows women can do and be anything tells the
story of Mary Magdalene and the resurrection of Jesus. All of the Scriptures about
the resurrection mention that women were the first witnesses on the scene. This
is a really big deal. It was believed at that time that the words of women didn't
matter. Women could not testify in court. It didn't matter if a woman was an eye-
witness or just had really important stuff to say. It was believed that her words
would be unreliable or inaccurate, just because she was a chick!

So the biggest story of all time and, in my opinion, the most significant element of our faith—the resurrection of Jesus—was revealed first to women, and their testimony mattered more than anything had ever mattered in the history of important things.

If the resurrection of Jesus wasn't real, if he didn't come back three days after he died, if we don't serve a risen Lord, then none of this Christianity stuff matters. If Jesus didn't really have power over the grave and death, then it's all a fraud and he really was just a good teacher and not the Savior of the world.

So the fact is that, in God's rock star plan for the beginning of his church, the most important truth came from women. This destroys any separation of women from God, or the elevation of one gender over another. Just like when the veil in the Holy of Holies was torn—symbolizing that anyone could go to the Lord in prayer—in this same way, any barrier that kept women down was torn. Now we can proclaim the truth of Jesus to any and to all! That's kind of a sweet deal.

This works out really well for me, because I HATE being told that there is something I can't do. Friends in my life can vouch that I say often (and sometimes in anger), "I DO WHAT I LIKE!"

You ready to hear something crazy? I love rules. I know, I know; that sounds like it's "opposite day". But really, I love living and operating when there are clearly defined rules in place. Because when there are clearly defined rules and standards, we have the freedom to operate any way we want inside those boundaries. There is no confusion regarding what is acceptable or what you may or may not get in trouble for. There are few things worse than wondering if you're gonna get in trouble for something and not knowing if it's gonna really upset someone. That's not to say you won't ever make people angry, especially if you are doing new things, or if people wish they had the courage to do what you're doing; you're almost guaranteed to tick off those folks.

Some people may put unnecessary shackles on you and, in times like that, it's okay to contest those kinds of messed up boundaries. If no one challenged the standards of the day, then we wouldn't have Martin Luther King Jr., or Malala Yousafzai, or Jesus, or Mother Theresa, or Nelson Mandela, Fanny Crosby, Bono, or maybe even you and me. There will be times when we have to fight the man for the greater good. Be ready for those times.

We all have different personalities and goals, which is cool because if we were all the same, very little would be accomplished for the kingdom, and there is a good chance we would end up killing each other. So I know that not everyone who reads this will have the same view as I do. But speaking for myself, I want to be a warrior.

I am a fighter and I want to charge in headfirst, fully committed and knowledgeable about anything that God puts in my path for me to accomplish. I want to finish what I start, I want to create positive change in our world, and I don't want to be anyone's sucker in the process. That's not too much to ask or expect of ourselves, is it? This is not an exclusive desire for girls. But this can be a harder concept for girls to get behind than it is for guys.

From when we are little, boys play with blocks and create things, or weapons and celebrate triumph over another whenever they can. Girls play with dolls and make sure they look cute while doing it. But what about the girls who grow up and don't want to do what people have always told them they are supposed to do? What if they are leading the charge to change injustice in our world as warrior queens instead of pretty, pretty princesses?

There was a specific time in my life when I knew that I was different. Before I went to church at The Salvation Army, I went to another church that shall remain nameless. I was twelve-ish and in a youth group with a bunch of other girls. I'd been going for a few months and was starting to feel like this may not be the best place for me. The day I went to what would end up being my last time at that church, we had a makeup party. (When you hear me say that I am a warrior and not a pretty princess, please don't hear me saying I don't like to look nice. I do, and I LOVE makeup—especially eyeliner. Lots and lots of eyeliner.)

So we were having this makeup party thing, which was cool. We all were using these mirrored dividers, which stood in front of us on the table so we could see what we were doing but no one else could see until we all put the dividers down for the big reveal.

We had all finished our faces, our leader counted to three, and we laid our dividers down and looked around. Every girl in the circle looked exactly the same. They had all done beige eye shadow and clear lip-gloss, and the lightest shimmery blush that ever existed. Every. Single. One.

Except for me. I wasn't used to using makeup so I wanted to go all the way and incorporate all of my favorite colors. I did bright blue eye shadow from lashes to brow, blush that was nearly purple, and orange lipstick. They all looked just like they had before, and I sat there looking like an embarrassed circus clown, but no one was laughing. My insides were on the outside. People could see that I was different from the rest, and I realized that I wouldn't ever fit in this group. It was time to go.

I am thankful for this circus clown experience, because a few months later I went to The Salvation Army for the first time. One of the first things I noticed was this was where the warriors went to church. They may not have been wearing their blue eye shadow and orange lipstick, but they had their armor on and were not concerned about fitting in and being just like everyone else. The women were strong and showed there wasn't anything that they couldn't do.

I even had a single mom as my pastor. This placed rocked, and I was home.

Ladies reading this, I hope you know that you can do whateva you want to do. Preach. Teach. Paint. Fix things. Be an amazing mother. Be a good boss. Design buildings. Tame lions. Be an untamed lion. Be successful. My sincerest prayer is that we realize the freedom and potential we have in Christ, and are women who encourage other women.

Sometimes we get the idea that there can only be one strong woman, and it has to be me. We get jealous of other women who are doing great things too. Don't be so insecure that you put others down to ensure your space as queen bee.

The strength of a confident community of believers is our greatest asset in making major change in our world, and in welcoming more people into the body of Christ. So rise up as women who love Jesus and each other. Support and encourage each other as we build up the kingdom. Be a warrior—whatever that looks like for you—and keep fighting for what matters most.

Questions for Reflection:

•What are some Scriptures that confirm that women can do great things for Jesus?
•Has there ever been a time when you felt like you were treated as a second-class citizen because of your gender, or maybe for another reason?
•How will you be a warrior?
•Who will join you in the fight?
•What are you afraid of?

"I Don't Care if the World Knows What My Secrets Are"

"I don't care if the world knows what my secrets are. So what?"

These are the lyrics of the chorus of one of my favorite songs. They are by a singer/songwriter named Mary Lambert. I was driving when I heard this song for the first time, and I will never forget how those lyrics made me feel. There are a ton of things that I love about this song. But when she said she didn't care if the world knew what her secrets are, it kinda blew me away.

Really? You really don't care if people know all your dirties? You would shout them from a mountain top and not even freak out a little bit? That's brave.

Some of us would do anything to keep our secrets hidden. Anything. End friendships. Lie. Leave big parts of our lives out of conversations. Move. Run. Anything.

I like my secrets. If I keep them to myself, they keep me safe and hidden and guarded. If you don't know my secrets and decide you don't like me, that's okay because you didn't really know me, you didn't know all about me. But what if you saw all the things I work hard to keep hidden, and you loved me anyway? Everything would be different. Everything.

I taught a class once at a big youth leaders' training event about how to counsel a teen or young adult who is struggling with sexual identity. Teaching this class was probably one of the most challenging things I've ever done. Leading up to it, I did a lot of reading and studying. For six weeks straight, every day I looked into books, talked to wise friends, prayed and even cried. I think I cried more during my time of study and preparation than I've cried at most major events in my life. I searched and searched for a clear answer. The "answer" that kept coming up for me was that this was not as obvious as we all want it to be. This is a person's life, and if you are trusted enough for someone to come to you with this heavy secret, you should feel honored and realize the gravity of it before you decide anything.

The best way I could think to show my class how huge of a deal this was and to help them realize this wasn't an "issue" or a "debate," but a person whose life could be destroyed if they chose to misuse the information, was to do the same thing right then. I knew that I was going to have friends in that room who could use for this life-changing object lesson.

So I called my great friend K.B. Hall up to the front. In hindsight, I probably should have given her a little head's up, but where's the fun in that? I have known

K.B. since 2003, and she is one of God's best gifts to me. I asked her a few questions at the front of the room to show that we were good friends and didn't just make up this story right before class started. Here is how the hardcore part went down. (Also, I call her Beesha; that's her hood name.)

> Me: Beesha, I would say that we are really great friends. Are you with me on that?
>
> Beesha: Yeah, for sure.
>
> Me: So because we are really good friends I am going to tell you a secret. This is a secret that I've only told my husband, and maybe one other person. I hope that after I share it with you we can still be friends, and you won't look down on me.
>
> Beesha: There isn't anything you could say that would make me not want to be your friend anymore.

Here it comes.

> Me: K.B., I am in recovery from an eating disorder. It has been a part of my life since I was nineteen years old. There were times when I felt like it would be the end of me. There was a season in my life when I felt like it was closer than my skin, and during the times when I hated myself for being a fat bulimic, I felt like I was the definition of a failure. I couldn't even have an eating disorder right. I'm getting better, and I've been better for a little while. And part of me getting better is letting this secret out. I hope that you won't look at me any differently.
>
> Beesha: I still love you. Nothing's changed. I hope we can talk about this more in the future.

We hugged it out in front of about sixty people, and I moved on with the class.

It is rare for people to share moments like this that are clearly sacred. Things like, "We lost the baby. I am a bulimic. I have cancer. I think I might be gay. He proposed!" All of these are tiny instances, a second or two in time when we decide to use words to give our news or our fears life. Being a part of that conversation is a sacred bond, no matter what comes next. If we prostitute that moment and make it about ourselves and our own opinions, then we have just spit on a God-given opportunity to be the body of Christ for one another.

I had a chance during that class to release the dragon that I'd been wrestling with for years. Its talons had dug deep past my forearms and into my soul. We tousled and fought for almost a third of my life but in that moment, as we were spinning in our last battle, I let go of my grip and realized that I was holding on to it as much as it was holding on to me. It was almost as if I could see its black webbed wings flap away as it flew into the horizon.

I still think about that dragon, and some days are harder than others. But letting it go brought freedom I hadn't ever expected. Honestly, when I told Beesha my secret that day in the workshop, my main intention was to have a really great illustration. It was all true, but I thought that if I dropped that bomb, it would prove my point. I think it did, but so many more unexpected things happened from there. Straight away I felt free and whole. So many girls came up to me after that class and told me that they had the same struggle. One told me that if I could be healthy, then maybe she could too. Another told me she is called to be a pastor in The Salvation Army, but was holding back because she had an eating disorder in her history, and she was sure it would be a deal breaker. This healing was the conformation she was waiting for to pursue her calling.

"I don't care if the world knows what my secrets are." How many things in our world would be different if that were really true? How many dragons would have no power? How many people would feel free for the first time? How many more apologies would be spoken without embarrassment? How many relationships would be reconciled? How many people could tangibly experience the grace of Jesus because the weight of guilt and shame would be gone?

We even try to keep our secrets from God. We think that if we don't pray about them, or talk about them, or act like they exist, then no one will ever know—not even the Lord. When we give those thoughts real words, it's crazy. We know that God knows it all. He sees our dragons for what they are, things that separate us from him and what he has for our lives. He hates our dragons even more than we do.

He already knows, friends. And he is ready with his arms open to help you find freedom and hope—the freedom and hope that Jesus died for you to live in every day. You don't have to be pretty and polished and have it all together for Jesus to love you.

Take a second and think about the things you never ever want people to find out, things that you would do anything to keep secret. Maybe they are things that you did, and maybe they are things that someone else did to you. Friends, even at your very worst—covered by guilt and shame and fear and regret—you are the one Jesus died for. The "you" that you hate, and are sure everyone else would hate too if they ever really knew you, is the "you" that Jesus looked at with his eyes of love on the cross and said, "This is for you."

Yeah, Christ died for the whole world. We know that, all that John 3:16 stuff. But Jesus loves you enough—the ugly sin-covered you—that he would have gone to that cross just for you.

Take that gift and live in that freedom. No more dragons.

If you let your dragons go, if you find help from a friend or pastor or counselor, they can't hold you captive anymore. Join me in dancing in the freedom and hope of Jesus. It's real, and it's waiting for you right now.

Questions for Reflection:

- What are Scriptures that talk about freedom in Christ?
- Who can you go to this week and share a secret with?
- What is a dragon that has been holding you captive? What makes you afraid to let it go?
- What would be different if you weren't held captive by it anymore?
- What is your action plan to not let that dragon ever come back again?

Wounds

First thing's first: I am not a therapist. This chapter will not take care of all the emotional wounds you have for the rest of your life—but it might be a great place to start.

I have a story that can make people cringe. Most of the messy bits are in this book. After I've shared my story with others, some have said that with a story like mine, their histories are nothing in comparison. This might be my least favorite response. We move into a dangerous place when we start defining our value or the realness of our pain by comparing ourselves to others. Just because my pain was horrible for me, it doesn't mean that your pain wasn't just as difficult to endure for you—even though our experiences were very different.

The things in your life that have caused you pain are real. There will always be people who have it worse, but that doesn't mean that your stuff is inconsequential. When we open ourselves up and let people see our junk and our wounds, and they let us see theirs, we have a choice. We can compare ourselves against them, and leave feeling confused and sad—maybe questioning why the things that have hurt us have had such an impact. Or we can gain one of the greatest things sharing our stuff can bring to all parties involved: perspective.

Perspective in this case means knowing that other people hurt too. You aren't the only one who has wounds. Abandonment. Fear. Abuse. Humiliation. Neglect. Shame. We all have things in our lives that have caused us pain. No matter what yours have been, they are a part of your story and they shouldn't be ignored or pushed aside.

Before we can make any long-lasting change, and to keep those hurts from ruling our lives, or even having any kind of control, we have to accept them for what they are. If we don't, then those hurts can lead to life choices that we wouldn't ever want for ourselves. I think about addiction, promiscuity, depression, and all kinds of other things that are often born from wounds that are ignored and allowed to fester.

We see our junk for what it is. Then we stand up in boldness and tell those things that they aren't the boss of us anymore. You don't get to rule my life. You don't get to be the guiding force in how I make my decisions. You don't get to push me to treat others poorly. You were the bricks and mortar in the walls I built up around my heart, and it's time to tear you down.

I had a counselor once who changed my life. In one of our sessions I told her about a horrible childhood memory I had that would resurface whenever I felt scared or stressed out. In this memory I was about five years old and my mom and I were at her favorite drug house in the neighborhood. It was getting late and I fell asleep on the broken couch, which was covered in stains and cigarette burns. I remember the cigarette burns because the melted fabric felt like a cactus. I couldn't understand how this would be a comfortable resting place for anyone.

Anyway, I fell asleep out in the living room, but my mom didn't want to leave yet. So at some point she put me in the back bedroom. I woke up in the middle of the night in a room I never saw before. There was nothing in the room but a squeaky mattress. Literally. Just a mattress, no box spring or bed frame. No sheets, blankets, or pillows. No dressers or other furniture. No curtains or blinds. Just a disgusting old mattress, a beam of light from the streetlight outside, and a terrified five-year-old Lisa.

I wish I had the words to describe the amount of fear I felt at that time. I was alone and terrified. I hadn't ever been so scared in my whole little life. That was, until I thought about opening the door. I was scared in that skeezy room, but at least I was alone. No one was in there trying to hurt me. If I opened the door, who knew what kind of horrible mysteries were on the other side?

So I stood there for what felt like forever, crying, with my little shaking fingertips barely touching the doorknob.

I told the counselor this story and she advised me to change the memory. After thinking she was a little bit crazy, and maybe I should leave quickly before I caught any of that crazy, I listened to what she had to say. My counselor and friend told me to picture that memory, little Lisa in that room, and then picture adult Lisa sitting next to her, telling little Lisa anything she needed to hear at that time to be okay. Sounds crazy, right? But I trusted her, and sometimes you do crazy things with people you trust.

So I sat back and closed my eyes. I went to that place in my mind and I pictured adult Lisa talking to little Lisa. Little Lisa was afraid and abandoned. I sat next to little Lisa and started telling her that she was going to be okay. In my mind I said to little Lisa, *Lisa, I know you are scared now, but everything is going to be alright. It may not seem like it now, but your mom loves you. She is sick and can't take care of you like she wants to. One day things will be better, and you will be safe. Jesus loves you and he is here with you right now. When you are grown, life will be great, and this kind of life will be long gone.*

Once I saw my hurts for what they were, and made steps to heal, I became a different person. Those hurts didn't control me anymore. Before when I was afraid or stressed, I would have flashes of that horrible memory and how little Lisa felt at that time. Once I started healing, I replaced that memory with those words of affirmation. Now I only think about that horrible memory when I am telling my story of healing and redemption.

We all have wounds, and they look different for each of us. But no matter what you've gone through—as the result of your choices or the choices of others—you can heal those wounds through the grace of Jesus.

Like I said, it is important to acknowledge those hurts for what they are. But it is equally important to make the decision that you can be okay; to make the choice to work toward healing; to know that those hurts will not define you, or be the "why" behind what you do and how you treat others.

I have had some pretty horrible stuff happen to me, but I am no one's victim. I refuse to stay in that place of pain or shame. I am redeemed and restored and renewed, and so are you—if you choose to let Jesus do what he came to do, to enter your life and change you for the better.

1 Corinthians 1:26-31 from *The Message* says: *Take a good look, friends, at who you were when you got called into this life. I don't see many of "the brightest and the best" among you, not many influential, not many from high-society families. Isn't it obvious that God deliberately chose men and women that the culture overlooks and exploits and abuses, chose these "nobodies" to expose the hollow pretensions of the "somebodies"? That makes it quite clear that none of you can get by with blowing your own horn before God. Everything that we have— right thinking and right living, a clean slate and a fresh start—comes from God by way of Jesus Christ. That's why we have the saying, "If you're going to blow a horn, blow a trumpet for God."*

God can use our wounds and hurts to bring him glory. When the world looks at what we've been through, they may say, "Of course they ended up addicts, or in jail, or with less than stellar legacies; look at what they've been through."

But I don't want anyone to say that about me. I want people to say, "God must be real! Look at what she's been through! After all that, she has hope and is helping others. I want what she has."

I still have hurts and wounds I am working toward healing. And as much as I hate to admit it, I have caused others hurt. But God is not nearly finished with me yet. Though it has chips and dents, I stand tall in my busted armor as a warrior for the cause of Christ and his kingdom—a victor, and not a victim.

Will you choose to stand with me, letting your battle armor shine?

Questions for Reflection:

- What are other verses that talk about who God uses for his glory?
- What wounds are getting in the way of you being who you were created to be?
- Are there conversations that you need to have with those who have wounded you, or maybe conversations you need to have with those you have wounded?
- You may need to get some help in this process from a pastor or counselor. There is no shame in that. If you do need an outside voice, who will it be, and when will you contact that person?

Create

I create. I make things. I paint things. I mold things. I make new things out of nothing. I start things, and sometimes I don't finish things.

I give things. I keep things. I send things, and sometimes I lose things.

If I'm not creating I feel like I'm not living.

It can be difficult for me to let people know how much I care about them, or for me to express that I am thinking about them or praying for them. But if I send you a bracelet or a painting, then maybe you will see that I do love you, and I think you are worth the time and effort it took to complete that thing you are holding, that you are special and valued. I can't do this for everyone, but if I've done it for you, I would hope you would see my life is better with you in it. You are important.

There are some days when I feel like I am nothing. Days when I feel like I can't get anything right, that I won't leave a legacy that matters. Then I paint. If no one remembers me, maybe they will remember my art. And whatever that painting means to them or makes them feel will be the difference they needed to have a better day than I was having.

I love to talk, but some days I have no words. I have nothing to say, and no one to say it to. But if I crochet a purse out of plastic shopping bags, I will know that even rubbish can have a second chance at being useful and beautiful.

On days when I'm full of joy I will sometimes create something you can eat. The happiness I want to share comes in the form of cupcakes or cookies or soup or pasta or barbecue. Does it really matter what it is, as long as we are enjoying it together?

We can see life differently when we stop. STOP. Stop thinking. Stop worrying. Stop feeling angry or sad. Stop laughing. Stop going. Stop doing. Stop everything. It can be hard to hear the voice of God if we fill every minute of our lives with sound and action. We use the busyness to drown out anything we may not want to hear, but it can also shout louder than the voice of God trying to speak into our lives.

We can stop and be still in silence, but how long does that last? For me, not more than a few minutes—if I'm being generous. Here is a compromise. You don't stop and sit totally motionless and in silence, but you slow down and focus. The best way I can do this is by creating something.

Out of all the creative things I like to do, painting is probably my favorite. I create a workspace by putting a black trash bag over the dining room table so I don't get paint everywhere. (I am also wicked messy, and I don't want to think too much about being clean when I create. So instead I find a way for my messiness not to be destructive.) I start with a canvas in front of me and my eyes closed. What do I see? Sometimes it's something abstract, or something from nature, or a tattoo-inspired design—something that in some way expresses how I am feeling at that time—and I just start painting. Whatever feels trapped on the inside now has a chance to be set free. I am still and quiet. When you paint, you can't really think about work, or family drama, or responsibilities. You need to think about letting the inside show on the outside. You think about color theory and shapes. What comes first, the fill or the outline? What is the background going to look like and how are you going to get from one color to the next: fade, gradient, hard lines or white space?

You are fully present and your mind slows down and is much more silent than it usually is. This is when I can hear the voice of God much clearer than when I'm caught up in the busyness of life. This is when I can meditate on Scripture and the lessons that the Lord is leading me in. This is a time for reflection and peace.

In creating a painting (or jewelry, or sculpture, or a blanket, or a collage, or digital art, or whatever it is we are creating) we are able, even just for a brief minute, to see the canvas as the Creator sees. We want it to be beautiful. We want it to be loved. No matter what we make, in some way it is created in our image. Even if it doesn't turn out just the way we anticipated, it has our stamp on it.

I think that is how God views us too. Of course, he is a master designer and we are all novices in comparison. He created us just as he intended us to be. We have made mistakes, and maybe our canvases have been nicked or damaged along the way, but we can still see the stamp of the Creator in us. The divine spark lives within us, and no matter how our canvases look to others, there is nothing we can do to extinguish that spark. God looks at his creation and smiles. You, just as you are right now, make God smile.

I've been painting and drawing for as long as I can remember. I have made some nice pieces. Most include trees, anchors, and the colors red, orange, and yellow. Those are just my favorite things to paint. When I first started out, I made some horrible paintings. They looked like a four-year-old painted them in the dark.

So as you begin some new creative adventure, be ready to make some garbage. You will create things that you are embarrassed to claim as your own, and that is okay. When we are learning any new skill or ability, we have to be willing to make crap before we make beautiful things.

My son plays piano. He hates it. He wants to sit down at his keyboard and play his favorite song straight away, with minimal practice and effort. But that isn't how it works. To do anything well takes time and patience, hard work, and the knowledge that you will make plenty of rubbish before the beautiful things start showing up to the party.

Be okay with making garbage. It gets better. My solution: don't tell anyone you are going to paint, or whatever it is you are planning on starting. Just do it, and if it's ugly or wrong or embarrassing, then throw it away, or paint over it and start again. This is your process, and no one else needs to see the results until you are ready. Maybe people will never see the results, but the journey of quiet reflecting while getting there is way more of the point anyway.

We should show Jesus at every opportunity. No matter what we do, we should do it for the Lord. When you create, you can both see God and show God. While creating you can have quiet time with God and allow him to enter your mind and be an active part of what's going on. What you create can show God. I have a picture in my office that I painted that shows God in an extreme way. It is an oil painting I made of a woman in the middle of a storm-tossed ocean, holding onto a cracked rock that is in the shape of a cross. The waves are beating her, and her clothes are ripped and torn, but she is holding fast to that anchor which is Jesus. No matter what is happening in my life, I want to always hold onto Jesus. This painting serves as a reminder every time I look at it.

We can also show Jesus when we give our art away. Like I said earlier, nothing makes people feel valued like giving them something that obviously took time and effort to make. It says to the recipient: you are worth the most valuable thing I have to give—my time and my attention.

You can also sell your creative treasures to expand the kingdom. When we were in San Francisco, I hosted a craft fair and sold enough paintings to build a water collection tank for a Salvation Army school in Africa. I've also done a jewelry fundraiser to raise money for the anti-trafficking efforts of The Salvation Army in Las Vegas. SEEDS of Hope helps women who are trapped in sexual slavery escape their captors and start a new life. My creations helped people find freedom. That's a pretty sweet thing to be a part of.

When life seems like it's moving too fast for us to get our bearings and get it together, it may be beneficial to stop and create. Take some time to slow down and let Jesus in, and make your chaotic thoughts step out.

Part of 2 Corinthians 10:5 tells us, *we take captive every thought to make it obedient to Christ* (NIV). No matter what crazy busy chaos is happening in our minds, we have the ability to stop letting those things have control over us, and instead give our headspace back over to Christ. He can be the king of our minds just as much as he rules on the throne of our hearts and lives. Every thought can be made captive for Jesus, even if that thought is of a blue robot with a toaster torso. (That's my next idea for a painting—and Jesus can have that one, too.)

Questions for Reflection:

- What do you like to create?
- What have you wanted to create, but have never tried? What is stopping you?
- When will you next stop and make something?
- What are inspiring Scriptures about God as a creator?
- What do you assume God thinks about his creation now?

A Drunken Lie

Everyone drinks, right? It's really not that big of a deal. The "legal" drinking age is twenty-one, but that's just a suggestion, not a real law. It's only bad if you have a problem.

Lies. Tricky and deceitful lies.

Alcohol has the potential to destroy lives. That doesn't mean that everyone who partakes in a beer after work will become a drunk, but those people who do find themselves consumed by alcohol never began thinking that is where they would end up. Guaranteed.

Growing up where I did, everyone drank. Normally when we say "everyone," we don't really mean everyone. But as I look back at my childhood, every single person consumed alcohol, though in varying degrees. Parents drank. Teenagers drank. Parents drank with their teenagers. Seeing people passed out drunk was a regular occurrence. Even as an eight-year-old I knew that if you saw people passed out drunk, you stopped and turned them on their side. That way if they threw up while unconscious, they wouldn't choke on their vomit.

Alcohol was a part of everyday life. So was poverty. So was abuse. Some may say that those things aren't connected. I would disagree with that.

I remember the day I decided that I would not let alcohol have a part in my life.

On Mother's Day when I was in fourth grade, my class made a craft for our moms. Before when we did this kinda thing, I kept it for myself. Partly because I was a selfish kid, and partly because I didn't want to give my mom any sense that I cared for her. (Perhaps those reasons are the same.)

This year I thought, *Maybe this can be a fresh start for us. Maybe this gift will be like a peace offering.* The craft was a cup to hold ink pens. I'll never forget that craft. We took clay, formed it into little balls and stuck them around a plastic margarine tub. Then when the clay air-dried, we removed the plastic tub and fired the clay in a kiln. Mine was a pearly pink, and I thought it was the most beautiful thing I'd ever made.

The day I brought it home I was so excited to give it to my mom. I walked in the apartment, ready for the tide to permanently shift as a result of this gift. But my mom was nowhere to be found. She came up missing on the regular, so I had several places to look. After about an hour I found her at a neighbor's apartment. She was out-of-her-mind drunk, and I felt like my gift that was going to change things had failed already.

In a fit of tears I handed off the pen cup and ran home. I was there for hours before she came home. I thought, *Maybe I can just talk to her about how things are and how we can make them better.*

I approached her and asked if she liked the cup. She starting laughing and said, "No, but it doesn't matter. I dropped it and it broke. It's outside in the dirt." Then she went to her room and locked the door.

That was the day I realized that I was going to be on my own. All hope I had for things to be good with my mother was gone. I knew in some ways this was just a silly craft that had been broken, but to me it was symbolic of a failed reconciliation.

I knew for me to survive I needed to make a plan about who I was going to be, and how I was going to get there. The first step was alcohol needed to be avoided at all costs.

Not everyone has a mom like mine. Praise God for that. So not everyone has the hard and fast reasons I have for avoiding booze and drugs. Some people have grown up seeing folks drink a small to moderate amount and still hold onto their jobs, and maintain their relationships, and not abuse their children. That can happen for sure. But I plead with you, friends, to see there is a very ugly and destructive element to alcohol that is very real.

The people who have a problem with alcohol started with just one drink. They also thought it was fine, and they could handle it. Sometimes one drink is just one drink, but sometimes it isn't, and we should really ask ourselves if the risk is worth it.

I love to ask why. What's the purpose? What's our motivation? And if you are a person who wants to drink, I would like to challenge you to search your motives. I don't know of any good reason for a person, even one with no destructive history or personal problems with alcohol, to think that drinking is a good idea. Being sober, healthy, and whole will make you feel better than a drink ever will.

When we drink it lowers our inhibitions and helps us make bad choices even when we don't need assistance acting a fool. When we drink it intensifies feelings of depression, anxiety and shame—which all lead to more drinking.

Remember that you don't matter. Sometimes we make choices just for the good of others. It was a privilege when I worked with women in recovery. I would spend time with them during their first few days of clean time. I was able to stand next to them and say, "I live a dry life too. I'm with you on this journey." Even though I never had a "problem," I get to unite with people on the journey of sobriety and walk that life with them. That's a cool place to be.

So far we have mostly talked about drinking, but there are lots of other things people do to fill up the empty spaces in their hearts. Some people have sex or get real close to it so they will forget about the bad things happening in their lives. Or maybe they just want to think that someone—anyone—cares about them. Some cut or hurt themselves so that their feelings, which don't always make sense on the inside, can be a real thing on the outside. Some people eat their feelings. They turn to food to feel comfort or happiness, even if just for a brief moment before the guilt and shame of that catches up to them.

If you are guilty of any of these fake ways to deal with life (I am guilty—and thankful for grace, forgiveness, and a fresh start every day), then I encourage you to be brave enough to go deeper. Really talk about what's going on that makes you want to act out. Journal. Cry. Scream. Talk to a friend. See a counselor. Whatever it takes to find the healing that Jesus wants us all to dance in. Things will get better.

I don't need anything but Jesus. Food. Water. Shelter ... obviously. We all have basic needs. But some think that they need to self-medicate with alcohol, drugs, or all kinds of other destructive behaviors just to get through. Maybe life has thrown you some curve balls. Fair enough. Real talk, sometimes life can seem unbearable, and dealing with it isn't easy. Often, things hurt more before they get better. It's like cleaning out an infection, you may have to go through some pain to get to the root of the problem. It can be easier in the short term to dull our feelings and emotions with substances or behaviors than it is to address the issues and work on healing.

I get it. Those are all valid feelings. But through those hurts, Jesus is still in control. Jesus is much bigger than the wounds of this world. We don't need drugs or alcohol to ease the pain when we have the creator of the universe at our side.

Depending on what you've been through, you might need some extra help. There is no shame in that. But let's not fool ourselves into thinking we can find that "help" in these vices.

There is a passage of Scripture that really speaks about our motives when it comes to getting lit up. It's in Proverbs 23:29-33: *Who has woe? Who has sorrow? Who has strife? Who has complaints? Who has needless bruises? Who has bloodshot eyes? Those who linger over wine, who go to sample bowls of mixed wine. Do not gaze at wine when it is red, when it sparkles in the cup, when it goes down smoothly! In the end it bites like a snake and poisons like a viper. Your eyes will see strange sights and your mind will imagine confusing things* (NIV).

There are some things in the Bible that are debatable and maybe even a little gray; this isn't one of those things. God wants you to be healed and whole. Getting drunk, or even being caught up in any part of that lifestyle, isn't in his plan for anyone.

God has better things in store for you.

Questions for Reflection:

- Have there been times when you've felt like you "needed" to drink? What led to that?
- What would your life look like if you never drank again?
- Are there people you need to talk to about their drinking?
- What are some Scripture passages about drinking versus not drinking?

Color

I have a son. Anthony Edward Barnes. Ten years old. He loves Minecraft, Legos, and action movies. He is tall and smart and cares deeply for others. He has a white mother and a black father. He also has fair skin, blue eyes, and straight brown hair.

As we approached the Martin Luther King Jr. holiday this year, his mind was completely wrapped up in the meaning and significance of this day. He would ask me questions like, "If Dr. King didn't do what he did, would I be able to be friends with_____," or about what his relationships would be like with other family members, as we have people from all ethnic backgrounds in our family tapestry.

After answering these questions and many others, I told him that if Dr. King didn't do what he did, then Mommy and Daddy probably wouldn't even be together, and he wouldn't be here at all. He was dumbfounded. "But you both love each other so much, how could you not be married? How could we not be a family?" We talked about the struggle in our country and how rights that should have been standard had to be fought for, with many dying in the process. He looked at me with his big blue eyes rimmed with tears and asked how he fit into all of this.

For the first time he realized that as a biracial person the lines for him are blurred. This is especially true for those who do not appear to be multiethnic. What I said in response to this may have been the best moment in my parenting history.

The paraphrased version goes something like this: God has given him a superpower. He has a black father, but most people will never know that just by looking at him. There are some people who are ignorant and hateful and, if they had the choice, they would never choose to be friends with or even have a conversation with a black or mixed person. Those same people would have no problem inviting my son into their lives based on appearances only. Because of that, God has given him the superpower of changing people's minds. He has the ability to infiltrate just about any group of people and be the voice of love and reason and unbiased opinions. With a superpower often comes a secret identity. But Anthony does not have the Batman kind of secret identity where he does all he can to keep Bruce Wayne and Batman separate. More like the Iron Man/Tony Stark kind of secret identity; they are separate, but not really.

There are few things better in the mind of a ten-year-old boy than hearing he has a superpower and a secret identity. It is my hope for him that he realizes the true potential of what he has to offer, not just because of what is seen, but because of the content of his character and the hope he has for the future.

His story and the questions of how he fits in the mosaic of life are not unique to him. We can all understand what it is like. It is human nature to want to be included, and part of being included sometimes means aligning yourself with people who are like you. Maybe your friends look like you, or like the same things you do, or live where you do. That is all well and good.

I still do that. I'm kinda weird. I have tattoos and stretched ears. I pride myself on hanging out with all colors and races of people, but when I see a weird white girl I get a little excited and think, *Oh! She's like me. Maybe we can be friends. Maybe she will understand me.*

But a cool part of God's kingdom here on earth is deciding you won't only spend your time with those who are just like you.

Different people with different backgrounds bring different things to the table and together we can accomplish different things for God's service to others. Different is good. Differences shouldn't be ignored or excluded.

I have heard people, in an attempt to sound less racist, claim to be colorblind. That. Is. A. Joke. And an offensive joke at that. No one is colorblind. As soon as you see my husband and I, you notice straight away that we are different colors. Instead of ignoring that (or pretending to and probably failing miserably), let's be honest and celebrate our differences.

When I first met my handsome best friend, it was about a month before Thanksgiving. We dated, and when Turkey Day rolled around, he invited me to spend it with him and his parents. This was our first introduction, and I was sweaty-pit nervous.

As it got closer, I asked Ant, "So, what is Thanksgiving like at your house?"

He said, "It's really traditional. Turkey and traditional sides, loving parents and crazy uncles. It will be a great time." So we went and it was a great time. His parents were really loving, and his uncles were indeed crazy. But his idea of traditional and my idea of traditional were very different.

We had turkey and ham, stuffing and mashed potatoes. But there was also mac and cheese, collard greens, black eyed peas and other things that I loved and ate way too much of, but were not "traditional" in my mind.

Differences aren't always bad, and shouldn't be avoided. Sometimes our differences are silly little things that have little to no consequence in this world. But sometimes our differences are big things that can't be ignored.

I grew up in Salinas, California, with mostly Hispanic friends. I learned quickly that there are things that are different between white families and Hispanic families. When I went into a Hispanic household, it was important to go up to every person there who was my age or older and greet each of them personally.

You must shake hands and make eye contact as you say, "Hello. Nice to meet you." If you don't, you are a big, fat, disrespectful jerk face. But white folks are totally fine with one big group hello to everyone.

In the Old Testament, there were just two "races": Jews and Gentiles. Those who believed in God and those who didn't. The plan from the beginning was for the Jews to be a nation of priests, like a group of pastors, to minister to the Gentiles. But for the most part, the Jews got all proud about being God's chosen ones and hated on the Gentiles for not being good enough. So Jesus came and put the brakes on all that junk.

Ephesians 2:14-15 from *The Message* says: *The Messiah has made things up between us so that we're now together on this, both non-Jewish outsiders and Jewish insiders. He tore down the wall we used to keep each other at a distance. He repealed the law code that had become so clogged with fine print and footnotes that it hindered more than it helped. Then he started over. Instead of continuing with two groups of people separated by centuries of animosity and suspicion, he created a new kind of human being, a fresh start for everybody.*

Things that divide and separate don't need to. We can acknowledge what makes us different from each other, but those things don't need to cause strife or animosity. Though we are different, as we do the whole Golden Rule deal—do unto others as you would want them to do to you—we can be kind and loving, even as we are honest about our differences.

Questions for Reflection:

- Has there been a time when you felt discriminated against?
- Has there been a time when you weren't as kind as you could have been because of
- something you saw on the outside?
- How would the world be different if we really treated people the way that we want to be treated?
- What are some Scriptures about unity and kindness in the body of Christ?
- What will you do if you see someone being belittled or discriminated against?

Tattoo Evangelism

"I use my tattoos to evangelize." Have you heard this before? I have, and I think it might be one of the dumbest things in the history of Christians trying to justify doing what they want under the guise of it being for Jesus' sake. Kinda like the crusades, with less blood. Still some blood—but less.

I obviously don't have a problem with tattoos. I currently have ten tattoos, and there is a high probability I will add to that number. This is a personal choice, but a choice that still affects others, and shouldn't be taken lightly. People try to trap me—I mean ask me—what I think the Bible says about tattoos. There are some verses that are super debatable. Your body is a temple (1 Cor. 6:19-20); I haven't seen a temple that isn't decorated with pictures. There's also that verse in Leviticus 19 about not cutting your bodies, or tattooing them in mourning for the dead. Yet the verse before that reminds us not to round off the hair on our temples or mar the edges of our beards. Let's see how rigidly people start following that one. Beard trims for no one!

My first tattoo was of Kermit the Frog holding a Bible in one hand and giving a thumbs up with the other—and he has a wonky eye because I flinched. So because that's not in mourning for the dead, I'm golden!

But seriously, most of the verses people use to proof text what Scripture says about tattoos are debatable. But one part of this major life decision isn't up for debate: What does your mom say? I think the most biblically-based argument that isn't taken out of context is that of honoring your father and mother (Ex. 20:12). If your parents aren't down with you getting a tattoo, then you gotta respect that. I know that's not the answer most of us want to hear, but that's where I sit with it, especially if you are living in their house, or if they are financially supporting you. It may be a great opportunity to dialogue with them about it and find out why they feel the way they do, even if you don't agree.

Anyway, this chapter isn't supposed to be about if tattoos are biblically allowed or not; it's about people using the excuse that they get tattoos to evangelize to others. So let's get back to that.

I have seen on social media people posting about great opportunities to share Jesus because of their tattoos. I'm not saying that if you have tattoos, they can't ultimately lead to a conversation about Christ. Anything can lead to a discussion about Christ. "You got new shoes? Oh that's nice. Jesus took people's shoes off to wash their feet." (Okay, maybe not anything can lead to a discussion about Christ, but you know what I mean.)

But that can't be why we get them, or our main way of sharing Jesus.

If you want to get a tattoo and do not have a moral or ethical issue with it (can you believe it, some people still do?) then that is your choice. But keep in mind that because some people have serious problems with tattoos—even though you don't— they can still have an impact on how you are viewed and maybe on your professional trajectory. If you can't handle the judgment and repercussions that come from tattoos, it may not be worth it.

Let me tell ya, I have felt crazy judgment and condemnation because of my tattoos, and at times it's had a major impact on me.

There was one pastor who asked me if we could get together and talk when I moved to a new city. I was down and we met up later that same day. We said hello, and right out of the gate she told me that she didn't like me, didn't trust me, and wouldn't be letting any of her young adults or teens attend any events that I was putting on because she thought I was a bad influence because of my tattoos (and at that point I only had six).

Those words hit me in my gut like a sledgehammer. I like working with teens and young adults more than I like anything else, and for her to tell me that she didn't trust me with her people knocked me on my butt.

We sat together and talked for nearly two hours, and at the end she was crying and I prayed for her. By the end of the day she sent in her church's registration for our upcoming youth event.

The Holy Spirit moved in her heart (and mine too, because in my humanness, I thought of taking this conversation in a very different direction: the parking lot!) and since then our relationship is great. But I will never forget her words. They hurt, but I was thankful that she was brave enough to say them to my face, because most people who feel that way keep it to themselves, or better yet, privately roast you with their friends.

Anyway, the point is, if you want to get a tattoo, evangelism can't be the reason. If your life isn't evangelizing, then it doesn't matter what you permanently place on your body. If I can't share Jesus wearing long sleeves, we have a problem.

As Christians, we need to be willing to share Jesus all the time, even when it is scary or we don't know what the outcome will be. I was at the airport a few weeks ago and I sat next to a pilot who was reading his Bible. I asked him, "Reading anything good?"

He looked at me, visibly taking notice of my tattoos and stretched ears, and said, "It's good for some of us, not so good for others."

I was speechless (which is a rarity in my life) for a couple reasons.

First, the way he looked at me was SUPER condescending. How could he have the opportunity to share his faith, but instead choose to snub me? And the crazy cherry on the what-the-heck sundae was when I posted it on social media, people tried to justify why it was okay that he didn't share Jesus.

"Maybe he had flown the whole country and was really tired."

"Could it have been a gender thing? Guys and girls shouldn't have those kind of intimate conversations."

"Maybe he didn't want to get into a debate"

How crazy is it that we can defend not sharing Jesus when a perfect opportunity presents itself, but then make up an excuse to get a tattoo that has some obscure religious meaning. When I was eighteen and got my stupid Kermit tattoo, I really thought it had significant meaning. Turns out the meaning was that I was a dummy who made an impulsive decision. (I don't feel that way about all of my tattoos, just the Kermit.)

People need to hear the truth in love. We have it. Let's share it. No excuses and no cop outs. Romans 1:16 says, *For I am not ashamed of the gospel, because it is the power of God that brings salvation to everyone who believes: first to the Jew, then to the Gentile* (NIV).

When we think that we need to have any kind of gimmick or superficial introduction in order to share the greatest truth on the planet, then we may not have a real understanding of the life changing power of God's Word. It brings life and sets people free. It doesn't need you to look or feel cool enough to share it with someone who is seeking. It has enough substance all on its own.

It is for everyone. Not just the trendy kids, or the hipsters with their slouchy beanies and too skinny jeans, or the ones who are all tatted up. It is a saving gospel for all. Believe it has enough power to do that, with or without your tattoos.

Questions for Reflection:

- Sometimes people get tattoos to set themselves apart or show that they are different. What sets you apart and makes you different?
- What is stopping you from sharing Jesus with others?
- What's your plan to share Christ with someone this week?
- What are some Scriptures that give encouragement for sharing the gospel?

Comparison That Kills

I just had the best weekend of my life. Literally. The best ever. I exaggerate a lot, but this is not one of those times. As of the time of the writing of this chapter, I've never had a weekend as amazing as Super Bowl weekend 2015.

The hubs and I are friends with an amazing guy named Cameron. We met Cameron while we were pastors in San Francisco. When we met him, he was a youth pastor for a church in the city. Cam is an artist. Music, spoken word, and my favorite: street art. He is an off-the-charts talented graffiti artist.

He was in Phoenix this weekend because he's on a reality show called "Street Art Throwdown," repping his city, his awesome art, and most importantly his faith in Christ. Cam is the kind of dude I want to be when I grow up.

There was a competition going on as part of all the pre-Super Bowl festivities. Friends do all they can to support each other, so Anthony and I took the kids to hang out for the competition. We were there for about four hours just watching Cam paint and chatting with all the other folks who were a part of what was going on.

One of the people there was Justin Bua. He is a producer and co-host of the show. Bua is an artist. But not just any artist, Bua is legit my FAVORITE artist. I have his stuff on my walls both at home and in my office. When I first started painting, I was inspired by a lot of his stuff. Not saying that my art is like his, because it's not at all. But his was so beautiful and evoked so much emotion that I couldn't help but create art too.

While the competition was happening, I was able to talk to Bua for a few minutes. I gushed about how much I love his art, and all kinds of lame fan girl stuff that I just couldn't really contain. We got a picture together, and I spent the rest of our time there trying not to let him catch me staring at him. (I failed at that.)

The competition finished and we were getting ready to dig out to get some dinner with Cameron. We were talking about where we wanted to go, and how quickly we could get away from the crowds and the cameras. Mid-conversation, Bua comes up and says, "Hey, are you guys going to dinner now?" We told him we were and he asked, "Would it be cool if I came with you?"

In my mind the world froze. *Is this really happening? Is one of my creative idols asking to come to dinner with me? Is this real life? Did I make up another crazy story again, and confuse it with reality? No. This is really happening. Whatever happens next Lisa, play it cool. Don't freak out on Justin Bua. That's not a good look.*

I responded like it was all no big deal, "Yeah, sure. You can come along." But on the inside I was hyperventilating and dancing and air punching with more excitement than I've ever had at one time.

Anthony and I walked with our kids, Cameron, and Justin Bua to our car and drove together to a nice, chill restaurant by our house.

We chatted a little, but I ended up not talking too much because I also felt like the extreme emotions inside my brain might make me vomit on Bua's lap. I had to choose between using words or keeping my composure. I chose composure, for the most part.

Bua started chatting with my son. My boy told him that he loves art too, and here comes the best part: Bua and my son drew a tandem picture together. Bua drew some on this erasable board the restaurant provided, then passed it to Little Ant to draw some, and this went back and forth a few times. I got a few pictures of this process, and was in awe of what was really going on.

I don't think my boy totally understood how big of a deal this really was, but I'm sure he will one day. Maybe when Little Ant has one of his paintings in a Bua gallery, they can reflect on this moment and laugh together.

As I was looking for the waiter to let him know that I was going to keep that board, and to ask how much I could pay them for it, I glanced at Little Ant just in time to see him erase the whole thing with his napkin.

My heart sank. I asked in horror, "WHAT ARE YOU DOING?" and he said, totally calm and unaware of the gravity of what he had just destroyed, "What Mom? We were done and I wanted to draw something else."

Kids.

Oh well, I have some cool pictures of it all.

We finished our meal and took the guys to their hotel for the night. I was in shock about the whole thing. I literally stayed awake until 4 a.m. staring at the ceiling, thinking about all that had happened, and how mind-blowing it was.

The next day we hung out with Cameron all day and watched the Super Bowl together. I was still flying high on all the excitement, and was thankful for the conversations we were able to have about faith, and art, and loving others. It was a day full of what Christian community really should be—not caught up in talking mess about others, or making fun of things that we don't love.

Being around crazy talented artists for two solid days inspired me to create some art. When I say inspired, I really mean that I felt like I wouldn't be able to function if I didn't paint. I had some art in there that I had to let out.

I stayed home with my two-year-old daughter on Monday and we painted together all day. I painted and looked at pictures of Cameron's stuff from the day before, and at Bua's paintings that are on my wall in the living room. Then a dark cloud came and surrounded me.

———

At the expense of sounding like a total diva, I am going to confess something. Most of my friends are not artists. Not that they can't make art, they just don't. Because of that, I am usually one of the best artists in my circle. But that day as I painted, I started to think the things I had made, things that I used to think were really good and brought joy, were garbage. Absolute trash. How much time had I wasted thinking that this was even worth it?

My stuff will never be as good as Cameron's or Bua's. Before that day, I never compared my art to anyone else's. I thought it was pretty good, and I loved doing it. That day I held my painting of giraffe silhouettes up against Bua's "The Poet" and felt like an idiot and a failure. I sat on the ground and sobbed.

Make a careful exploration of who you are and the work you have been given, and then sink yourself into that. Don't be impressed with yourself. Don't compare yourself with others. Each of you must take responsibility for doing the creative best you can with your own life. (Gal. 6:4-5 MSG).

I am no Cameron Moberg or Justin Bua, but I am a decent artist. When we compare ourselves to others, when we hold our painting of the giraffe up to "The Poet," we will always be left wanting.

It's human nature to want to be the best. I think that's probably why God's Word talks so much about the danger of pride and self-righteousness. Pride is a divisive demon that wants to kill and destroy. If I listened to that demon, I would probably never paint again. I would risk not using my passions and gifts for the glory of God because I'm not Justin Bua—and that is cray!

We don't have to be the very best at something for it to still be worth it. You may not be the very best preacher ever, but your words still matter. Share the gospel anyway. You may not have the most money or resources; give anyway. You may not be the best musician; sing anyway. You may be new to the faith, but you still have a valuable part to play in all of this. What you do matters.

Let's not hold on to the comparison trap, because it only leads to defeat. Instead, let's choose to dance in our own skin and rejoice in the gifts and passions that the Lord has given us, and serve him with every bit we have.

Questions for Reflection:

- Can you think of a time when you felt stunted by comparing yourself to others?
- Is there something you stopped doing because you didn't feel like you were good enough?
- What are some encouraging Scriptures that speak to this struggle?
- What is something you can do today that will express your creativity or passions in service that you may keep hidden?

Judge Me

"Don't judge me."

"Before you judge me, make sure you are perfect."

"People look at the outward appearance, but the Lord looks at the heart" (1 Sam. 16:7 NIV).

And my favorite, "Only God can judge me."

These are all sayings people use when it comes to "judging" others, and most are used incorrectly, including the Scripture. I do agree that assuming that you are better than others, or that God loves them less, isn't okay, but often it seems like people use the phrase "judging" when it's really not that at all.

Let's check out some Scripture about it: *"Do not judge, or you too will be judged. For in the same way you judge others, you will be judged, and with the measure you use, it will be measured to you. Why do you look at the speck of sawdust in your brother's eye and pay no attention to the plank in your own eye? How can you say to your brother, 'Let me take the speck out of your eye,' when all the time there is a plank in your own eye? You hypocrite, first take the plank out of your own eye, and then you will see clearly to remove the speck from your brother's eye"* (Matt. 7:1-5 NIV).

No one likes to be put down or insulted. When we feel like someone is on our case about something that doesn't really matter, we may feel backed into a corner, like we are being judged or belittled or defined by the issue of the day. We all have opinions and we all think we are right. Sometimes we are, and some things are debatable. Except for you. You're right all the time. (Insert sarcastic face here.)

The judging that Jesus is talking about in this chunk from Matthew isn't about when someone tells you she doesn't like your hairstyle or the kind of clothes you like to wear. It's not even about tattoos or piercings, or the kind of music you like. Jesus is talking about when we see other people's faults or differences and decide that we are better people than they are. Some seem to go to the point of thinking, *Because of our differences, and because I am right and they just aren't, it looks like they are gonna burn up in hell for all eternity. Let's all point and laugh.* Have you ever thought people felt this way about you? I know I have.

Hell is for real. We need to make sure that we are walking so closely with Jesus that we don't ever have to worry about hell being in our future. We should try to make sure that all those in our lives aren't going there either.

Jesus doesn't want us to look down on anyone as being a lesser form of human. He died for us all, even the ones who sin differently than you do, or maybe make choices that make you uncomfortable.

The Judgy McJudgersons are not exempt from this either. There is a good chance that someone treated them with judgment or contempt, so they feel the need to pass that ugliness on to others. We all have junk in our lives that has led us to live and treat others the way we do. Not to justify being a jerk, but sometimes perspective into others' lives can help us understand why we may need to be extra gracious.

This Scripture talks about what to do if you see people with debris in their eyes. There are a couple important things that we should unpack:

You see someone with a splinter in his eye. But this isn't just anyone you see walking down the street. This isn't a stranger. This is a brother. Maybe a brother by blood relation, but most likely a brother in Christ.

We get into a weird place when we try to "speak truth into someone's life" (I put that in quotes because some say that as an excuse to spit venom and rudeness, all in the name of Christian love and kindness), especially if we haven't earned the place to say those things. If I don't know you in a way that has led to close conversations about life and faith, please don't come at me sideways trying to fix what you don't like in me. This is often when you hear the "Don't judge me," or the "You don't know my life!" statements made in anger. I know I say them.

You BOTH have stuff in your eyes, but you, the one with the huge 2x4, go to the dude with the tiny splinter and try to point out what's wrong in his life. Many people ignore what's really going on in their own lives but, in an attempt to hide that 2x4, they have no problem letting others know what they are doing wrong. Real talk, the guy with the splinter might really need some support. Maybe that tiny splinter is messing up his life. He might even be desperate for a friend, a brother, to come along and offer some help and encouragement. But before we can do anything for anyone, we need to be honest about where we are, and what we are struggling with. This doesn't mean that you have to be perfect before you can help someone else, but you do need to be actively working toward holiness. (Sometimes that means doing the best you can with what you have and making every attempt to live tomorrow with more fight for justice, love for others, and desire for God than you did yesterday.)

When I was in high school, I had a friend who was having sex with her boyfriend. She was a Christian, and she knew this wasn't God's best choice for her life. One day at lunch she asked if we could "talk." Sidebar: if you aren't aware, at any age, across any time period, if a female human asks you to "talk," it is never about how great you are, or how glad she is that you are friends. If someone asks you to talk instead of just talking, it's probably a conversation that is going to suck—at least a little. End sidebar.

So we sat down at one of the tables and she started to tell me that she felt like God didn't like it that I had pink hair, and it sent off the wrong message.

I. Lost. My. Mind.

This chick had some nerve. Talk about a plank and a splinter. She had a major sin in her life, but it was something that she could keep secret and escape any kind of accountability about. Yet she came to me to have a "talk" (see, I told you those usually don't end well) about my pink hair? To be very clear, having crazy-colored hair is in no way a sin. It's a personal choice that has no bearing on our relationship with God or our ability to share Jesus with others. You may not like it, and that is fine. You are entitled to your opinion. (It is wrong, but you can have it just the same.)

Scripture tells us that once we have addressed the 2x4 we have lodged in our heads, then we go back to our brother and together work on his splinter. I don't know about you, but it wouldn't work well for me if someone came to me (even if it was someone I loved and cared for who had earned the place to call me out), dropped a bomb by pointing out my splinter, and then just left and expected me to be alone in that struggle. A great part of being in the body of Christ is that you aren't just a hand suspended in space. You are connected to other parts of the body to go through life together, even the rough bits that are ugly and uncomfortable.

For this to really work we have to genuinely care enough about people to call them out on their garbage. We have to love each other enough to see the splinter for the dangerous thing it is, and care enough to stop it before it spreads. This isn't for wimps. It's not for people who are afraid of confrontation or hurting someone's feelings. If we were friends and you saw me making decisions that could lead to destruction, I would hope that you would love me enough to pull me out of the pit before it swallowed me whole.

We need to be real about the negative, but on the other side, let's also be real about the positive. Just a few verses down the road in this chapter it talks about identifying who people really are, based on the fruit they produce.

Matthew 7:15-20: *"Beware of false teachers who come disguised as harmless sheep, but are wolves and will tear you apart. You can detect them by the way they act, just as you can identify a tree by its fruit. You need never confuse grapevines with thorn bushes or figs with thistles. Different kinds of fruit trees can quickly be identified by examining their fruit. A variety that produces delicious fruit never produces an inedible kind. And a tree producing an inedible kind can't produce what is good. So the trees having the inedible fruit are chopped down and thrown on the fire. Yes, the way to identify a tree or a person is by the kind of fruit produced"* (TLB).

We shouldn't be so afraid of "judging" others that we let our friends get sucked into a pit of sin and despair. It's not about saying we are better, it's about being together in the struggle.

We need to be checking out the kind of fruit people produce to really know what's going on. If they say that they are Christians but hate others, or don't show Jesus in anything they do or say, then maybe they aren't really what they claim to be. We should be just as concerned about their salvation as we are about our friends who don't know the Lord at all.

To strengthen the body of Christ, let's spend less time being concerned about not judging others, and more time being honest and loving followers of Jesus who aren't afraid of being fruit inspectors. Do we care enough to call each other out when we need it?

Questions for Reflection:

- Has there ever been a time when you felt judged or belittled? What was that like?
- Have you ever had the experience of having someone you love and care for call you out when you needed it? What was that like?
- What are some Scriptures that talk about unjustly judging?
- What are some Scriptures that talk about being fruit inspectors?

Wild Things and Unloveables

If you catch me in a bar where the wild things are
With my pastor and an entourage who loves God
Please don't think that it's odd, we kick it 'round broken hearts
Fishing for men, surrounded by sin but ain't taking part
I talk about Jesus, all the Christians love me
I walk like Jesus now they wanna judge me, ain't it funny?
I'm ducking stones thrown from the Pharisees
Gospel of Peace up on my feet like a pair of cleats
Walking with the Paraclete, that's Greek for The Spirit
They say the wild things'll eat you up
Who shall I fear when God is walking with me
If I die that's a win, that's the seed of the church plus I get
to be with Him
And we so undefeated like Hanes made our sneakers
I had beef with Jesus and my sin it got deleted
So I gotta go and speak it to those who really need it
Let the Gospel off the leash, go and be where the beasts at
I wanna go where the wild things are
I'm talking lions, tigers, bears (oh my)
Christ died for the terrible heart
That's why I wanna be where the wild things are
—Andy Mineo, "Wild Things"

This is a song that talks about wanting to go and be amongst people who desperately need Jesus. People so caught up in a life of sin and sadness that they see no other way to live, no hope for anything better, and maybe even no idea that things could ever be different.

These are the folks who might make you feel uncomfortable. And in some cases, that might be justified, especially if they are living it up, taking part in illegal activities. In other cases, they may just need one person to show them that there is another way to live, a way that doesn't bring harm to others or themselves. A way of life that is void of drama and full of peace. A life that helps instead of hurts, loves instead of hates, cares instead of ignores, restores instead of destroys and hopes instead of despairs. That example could be you. It could be me.

BUT THEY ARE FREAKS!

Yeah, they might be. But so what? Look at the people Jesus hung out with while he was here. Talk about freaks! Those dudes fit the freak job description fully. The people who Jesus spent a good chunk of time with were on the margins of society. He loved people who the world had decided were worthless. He loved us when we felt worthless.

One of my favorite chunks of Scripture is about the woman caught in adultery—John 8:3-11. Go read it. Like, right now. This book will be here when you get back. I'll wait....

Ok. So it's a good one, right? What Jesus did here was REVOLUTIONARY. By the law of that time, the woman should have been killed because they caught her having a get down with someone she wasn't married to. (Notice that the dude is nowhere to be found. But that's another rant for another time.) Make sure you see that Jesus not only saves her from literally being killed that day, but also from a life that is crippled by the oppression of bad choices when he tells her to go and leave her life of sin. That's the hinge pin of this whole story. Go and leave your life of sin.

And she's just one of the people who felt outcast that the Lord loved and encouraged and stood up for and called on their crap (see the previous chapter on how important that is). Let's make a short list of the wild things who hung out with Jesus. Take some time to look them up and see how countercultural Jesus was, and still is.

The prostitute with the perfume (Luke 7:36-50).

A crippled dude by the pool (John 5:1-15).

A bleeding chick (Mark 5:24-34).

That's just a couple. At the end I will challenge you to look for more examples of wild things and unloveables Jesus interacted with. Hint: there are tons.

There are people who are hurting and in need of Jesus. How will they see Christ if we don't show Christ? We need to go where the hurting are, but not at the expense of our own walk with God, and not with the intent to tell them that living tangled up in sin is totally okay.

If you are going to go into the trenches, your faith and walk need to be strong enough that you don't get swallowed whole and become a zombie just like them. Don't try to go and love on those in the margins, the outcasts and those who are trapped by their sin, if you aren't brave enough to stand up for the truth of God's Word. If you are likely to follow the herd, this dangerous territory may not be for you.

One of the best parts of my covenant as a Salvation Army officer says that I will "love the unlovable and befriend those who have no friends." Sometimes we have to go where they are to do what we say we are going to do.

I was a freak and a weirdo to the core. When I first started attending The Salvation Army as my church, the people there had every reason not to associate with me. I cussed, and lied, and stole, I put my hands on people in less than kind and courteous ways, and I even got drunk at my youth leader's house when she was out of town (sorry, Lorrie).

I was the textbook definition of a wild thing, but the church really loved me like Jesus did, and it changed my life forever. Maybe that's why I feel like I can relate so much to the woman from John 8. As soon as she started interacting with Jesus, she seemed to be expecting instant and eternal disapproval. Maybe that was the way everyone else in her life had treated her. Maybe that's all she thought she was worth. But Jesus thought otherwise.

If I'm being totally honest, I still kinda feel like a freak. Most of my life I've felt like I didn't fit in. I wish I could say that now that I am a confident adult this feeling is totally gone, but it's just not. I say this not to discourage you, but to let you know that the feeling of not fitting in may not totally go away. However, that doesn't have to be a bad thing.

Since we are already being honest and we are friends (we are still friends, right?), then I can say at this point in my life, I like not fitting in. I like being different and accepting the person God created me to be. I try to fake normal, but it just doesn't work for me. Being a weirdo who is totally confident in who I am in Christ, in my walk of holiness, and in my desire to serve God and the lost is a pretty sweet place to be. Sometimes, friends, when you and Jesus are tight, it's okay to let your freak flag fly.

Speaking of freaks, we can't mention weirdos and wild things without talking about William and Catherine Booth, the co-founders of The Salvation Army. They were super weird in their day, but the best kind of weird. (Please read the above chapter before you have me excommunicated.)

William Booth had a ton of great speeches and sermons that are quotable even to this day. I mean, "I'll Fight," come on! That's our anthem! My favorite William Booth quote is from a sermon called "Don't Forget" in 1910:

> I am glad you are enjoying yourself. The salvation business is a friend of happiness. Making heaven on earth is our business. Serve the Lord with gladness is one of our favorite mottos. So I am pleased that you are pleased! But amidst all your joys don't forget the sons and daughters of misery. Do you ever visit them? Come away and let us make a call or two.

Here is a home, six in family, they eat and drink and sleep and sick and die in the same chamber. Here is a drunkard hovel, void of furniture, wife a skeleton, children in rags, father now sleeping; the victims of his neglect. Here are the unemployed, wandering about, seeking work and finding none. Yonder are the wretched criminals cradled in crime, passing in and out of the prisons all the time. There are the Daughters of shame, deceived and wronged and ruined. Traveling down the dark and blind to an early grave. There are the children, fighting in the gutter, going hungry to school. Growing up to fill their parents' places. Brought it all on themselves, you say? Perhaps so. But that does not excuse our assisting them. You don't demand a certificate of virtue before you drag some drowning creature out of the water. Nor the assurance in a man of faded grace before you deliver him from the burning building. But what shall we do? Content ourselves by singing a hymn? Offering a prayer? Or giving a little good advice? NO! Ten thousand times no! We will forgive them. Feed them! Reclaim them. Employ them! Perhaps we shall fail with many. Quite likely. But our business is to help them all the same.

We can't follow this lead, and make positive changes for the kingdom, if we are so afraid of going where the wild things are that they stay lost and wild forever! Where would we be if someone didn't care enough to go to us in our most desperate time of need and show us the love and healing of Jesus?

If we are gonna go fight for and love the wild things, then we go in just wanting to show them Jesus, not with an agenda that devalues the relationship we may form with them.

I was at Starbucks one time and I starting talking to a chick there. We first started talking because I grabbed her drink thinking it was mine, took a sip and said in my loud and sometimes overly excited voice, "What is this garbage? It tastes like burnt hair!" Turns out it was her drink (and I think that soy milk in espresso drinks tastes less than favorable). The kind barista made her a new burnt-hair special and we sat together and laughed.

In this conversation we found out that we had a lot in common and decided to trade numbers and plan a day to hang out soon. Sarah (not her real name) and I hung out a lot and after we had known each other for a few months, she told me that she was a salesperson for one of those magic skinny pill diet supplement things. She then started to pitch me on selling it too, and when I kindly told her I wasn't interested, she got upset with me.

At the end of our last conversation Sarah said, "I really thought you would want to do this. It could make us both a lot of money. Why do you think I've invested so much time in hanging out with you?"

My heart sank. I really thought that she "invested" so much time with me because she wanted to be my friend. I was wrong. She had an agenda. She only wanted me in her life for what I could do for her, and in the hopes that we could both be in this type of "club" together.

When I tell this story, she seems like a weasel—and I'm okay with saying that she was. But how often do we do that same kind of thing as Christians? We befriend people, solely in the hopes that we can change them. We may feel like our motives are good, but if we care more about the end game than we do about the relationship and showing Jesus ourselves, then we are weasels just like Sarah.

I hope I never have a friend like that again. I hope I am never a friend like that again.

Questions for Reflection:

- What are other verses that talk about wild things or unloveables?
- What can you do to reach out to people who desperately need Jesus while still making sure your faith is solid?
- What can you do this week to welcome those who are different from you into the body of Christ?

The Christian Cage

Sometimes my least favorite thing about being a Christian is being around other Christians.

I said sometimes. This isn't an "all the time" feeling or even a "majority of the time" feeling. But SOMETIMES people who call themselves Christians are the worst folks to be around. I often refer to them in proper Lisa Barnes fashion as "the turd in the punch bowl." Nothing ruins the party quicker.

I chose my words very intentionally: people who call themselves Christians. There are people who have grown up in Christian homes and have Christian parents so they falsely carry the title of "Christian" themselves when they haven't accepted Jesus as an active and regular participant in their hearts and lives. They act like jerks and make us look bad. Most of these folks don't recognize that they are the turd in the punch bowl until they have had some major crisis and realize that they've been living without Christ this whole time.

The above-mentioned phony Christians are a more forgivable bunch because most of the time they don't even realize that they are living without the proper foundation of life and faith—a real relationship with Jesus and the guidance of the Holy Spirit. I'm not saying they get a free pass, but understanding that they just don't get it yet can help us be more gracious.

There is another group of phony Christians who are even more difficult to be around: the rotten fruits. These are the ones who are known for their jerk tendencies and hard hearts. These people at one time really knew the joy of the Lord. But, as time passed, something happened to them. I wish I knew what it was specifically, because then when I saw them unraveling I could scream, run, and create a diversion to spare their souls from this horrible way of living.

Whatever led to this life-sucking condition, they now have no evidence of an active relationship with Jesus. Their words are made of venom and thumbtacks. They take every opportunity to hurt others with their speech and actions. These are the folks I want to run away from as fast as possible. (Just in case you are trying to picture this, I run with the speed and agility of a person who is escaping a hurricane on roller skates; it's not pretty.)

A couple of chapters ago, I talked about how important it is for us to be fruit inspectors. We gotta look for characteristics in people that reflect Jesus. I want my friends to be reflections of Christ. I want to go to them when I'm struggling, and have the support and advice they give reflect the words and love of Christ. I want my pastors to have words that are seasoned with grace and love instead of gossip and discontent. That's the kind of pastor I wanna be too.

If you've spent time with "Christians" who aren't examples of "little Christs" (what the word Christian means), people who don't bear the fruit of living life with Jesus, then I would ask if they really are Christians, if they are saved. That's a big deal.

In The Salvation Army we have eleven doctrines that state what we believe as a movement. One of them is, "We believe that salvation depends upon continued obedient faith in Christ." So it's fair to say that to be saved and stay saved, you gotta have continued faith in Jesus. We all have seasons of doubt; that's not what this is talking about. It's talking about when we intentionally evict God's presence from our lives. As we have continued faith in Jesus, there is fruit of that in our lives; see the fruits of the spirit listed in Galatians 5 for examples.

So if we say we are Christians but have no fruit, we are lying. We are lying about our faith. We are lying about our character. And we are lying about our integrity. So friends, when you see someone who claims to be a Christian, but that person is fruitless or shows rotten fruit, then take action! This is too serious to stand on the sidelines and watch as people implode on the way to destruction. Even if they are mean and hurtful people. This is eternity business.

Care for the fruitless, pray for them and be honest with them about their walk with the Lord. But don't listen to them, don't take their venom and thumbtacks too seriously, and please do not let their bitter hearts bite you in the butt or change the way you view the real Jesus. He is a good dude who they don't know right now. The opinions of the fruitless don't always count.

There is another group of Christians I don't love spending time with. This one is much more about personal preference than a salvation issue, but this is my book and most of it is about personal preference. This is the group that I call "the oversaved." Only Christian things are allowed in their lives. Only Christian books, Christian friends, Christian activities, Christian music and the like. Again I'm not saying that these things are bad, but when you live in a purely Christian cage, you will have a very skewed view of the world. Old people would say, "So heavenly minded they are no earthly good," to describe how effective these folks are for Jesus.

I read Christian books, even some Christian nonfiction, and I like a good chunk of it. But it is strange to me that only Christians have a genre of writing dedicated to Amish love stories. That's weird.

I have Christian friends. Most of my friends are Christians, not "Christians" (but I do have some of those too—one of the hazards of the job), and they are imperative to my life and my larger-than-normal daily quota of laughter and texting funny memes.

Just as important as having Christian friends is having non-Christian friends. Salt and light! We gotta be it to a bland and hurting world. Not with an agenda, but with a genuine care for the lost, and the desire to show Jesus to those who have never seen him before.

Christian activities are also important aspects of our lives. Things like Bible studies, small groups and church youth groups are all great. But usually, only Christians go to those things. If we only hang out together, then how are we sharing the truth with those who don't know Jesus? I'm not suggesting we spend the rest of our free time going to the club or to a bar, but there are things we can do to expand our sphere of influence outside of the church walls. I'm thinking of things like book clubs, sports, or other volunteer and service opportunities.

There are people out there who would love to get to know you, and may even be interested in hearing about Jesus if you gave them a chance to see him in your life first.

For a long time, I thought I hated Christian music. Turns out, I just hate country music. Too bad these two genres often sound very similar. I do think that "Christian" should not be a genre of music. We don't classify any other genre of music based on the lyrical content. No one says, "I really love wild party girl music," or "hood guys making money music," or "sad breakup music." Seems dumb to me.

Music can be a great intro to conversation: "You like (insert your favorite singer or band here)? Me too! What's your favorite song?" INSTANT BEST FRIENDS! Ok, maybe not that intense, but you know what I'm talking about. There is good music that isn't riddled with foul language or women being objectified. (Super conservative folks, you might be surprised what's out there.)

If we spend all our time surrounded only by other Christians, we are missing opportunities to share God with people who have no idea about who he is. Maybe they have only known "Christians," and that's who they think we all are! Let's show the world that we are people who will meet them where they are and show the real Jesus in our actions.

If we are so wrapped up in Christian things and Christian music and Christian books, we could be missing an opportunity to find common ground with a new friend, before we can establish Jesus as our common ground.

Matthew 5:14-16 from *The Message* translation says it the best: *"Here's another way to put it: You're here to be light, bringing out the God-colors in the world. God is not a secret to be kept. We're going public with this, as public as a city on a hill. If I make you light-bearers, you don't think I'm going to hide you under a bucket, do you? I'm putting you on a light stand. Now that I've put you there on a hilltop, on a light stand—shine! Keep open house; be generous with your lives. By opening up to others, you'll prompt people to open up with God, this generous Father in heaven."*

Let's be public for the Lord. Let's be out shining for God in the dark places, not just a bunch of lights huddled together where we feel comfortable and safe. Let's be relatable and change the world, as shining lights for Jesus; real Christians, and not "Christians."

Questions for Reflection:

- How are you going to be light in a dark place this week?
- Are there areas of your relationship with God you need to increase before you step out in boldness in this way?
- Are there any "Christians" you need to call out in love and kindness about their fruitlessness?
- Spend some time in prayer and reflection on your own heart. Are there any areas you need to adjust to make sure you are honest and authentic about your faith?

A Love Letter to the Life Changers

You've made a difference in my life. I wouldn't be the same if it hadn't been for what you did for me. Thanks for loving me when no one else did. Thanks for showing up.

How would you feel if someone said any of those things to you? I would feel humbled and blessed and all warm and fuzzy on the inside if someone said anything like this to me and really meant it. When we look back at the junk we have gone through, often next to the junk we see someone who loved us, or was there for us when we really needed it. A life changer.

Many of my life changers have no idea what they did for me, or how much God really used them. It makes me wonder how different our communities would be if we were more honest about the parts people have played in the production of our stories, even the parts that were great tragedies.

There are a few people who were instrumental in my life. Without these people, I would be dead, in prison, or at least desperately hopeless. I have lots, but for the sake of time, and to keep from boring you too severely, I will only name a few.

Lorrie

The first life changer I ever knew was my first youth pastor, Lorrie Davis. I met her when I was fourteen and at the pinnacle of my craziness. She was in charge of all the youth stuff at The Salvation Army in Gresham, Oregon, and as I write this she still is—seventeen years later. That in itself is a huge statement, since most youth workers get burned out and dig out in two years or less.

Lorrie kept me in church when I wanted to run the streets. She was the first person who I knew loved me unconditionally. There was one day when my mom and I got in a huge fight. We were both punching and kicking each other. When my mom decided that her punches weren't enough, she ripped all the chords off the back of the TV and started hitting me with them. I fought for what seemed like forever. Then I felt all of the desire to fight leave me at once. I lay on the ground at my mom's feet, covered my face with my forearms and thought, *Either she is going to get tired and give up, or she is going to kill me. Either way, I can't fight anymore.* Thankfully she did get tired. My mom stopped hitting me, walked over to the couch, and just fell asleep like nothing had happened.

I made my way to a neighbor's house to use the phone (we had broken ours in the brawl). I called Lorrie and she came to pick me up. I didn't know it when I called, but she was at the movies. She took me to the theater and paid for me to watch the last ten minutes of *Flubber* with her and her family. As I sat there picking the dried blood out of my hair, I heard the voice of the Lord for the first time. I felt like God was saying to me, "Lisa, your family will never look like you want it to. Your mom will never love you or care for you like you should be cared for. But there are people in your life who will love you like family—and they will be enough."

I went to church for a while before I believed that God was real, and even longer before I believed that God loved me. But before I understood that God loved me, I knew that Lorrie loved me. If she could love me when no one else had, then I held out hope that maybe God could love me too. I was right.

Mark and Jo

I love summer camp! I spent four summers working at a Salvation Army camp in the redwoods of California. This place changed me in more ways than I can count. The most substantial way would be the friends and mentors I gained in Mark and Josephine Morton. They kept me on staff when they had just cause to fire me, because they believed I had potential. Or maybe because I was very funny and they liked having me around; I'm ok with either one of those reasons.

Before working with Mark and Jo, I never saw a marriage that seemed worth having. All the other examples looked miserable. The dude always seemed bored, or inconvenienced by his nagging wife. Or the wife looked belittled and stifled by a controlling husband. I thought if this was what Christian marriages looked like, I didn't want anything to do with them. But Mark and Josephine were different.

Mark loved Josephine with a kind and supporting love I'd never seen before. She is funny and outspoken. Mark never seemed embarrassed by her, or like he wanted her to keep quiet. I liked that. I knew that if I was ever gonna be married, I needed to find a dude who would let me be me.

Josephine's respect for Mark seemed motivated by her care and love for him. I liked that too. It seemed cool that you could treat your spouse like that because you wanted to, not because you felt like you had to in order to appease him.

After knowing them and observing their relationship for nearly five years, I met my handsome best friend, Anthony. I was still pretty freaked out by marriage, but because I saw the genuine love, care, and real happiness Mark and Josephine had, I thought there was a chance that I could have that too.

Jen

Jen Arens is an adult who expressed an interest in me from my late teens. I worked in San Francisco one summer running a day camp and the summer was coming to a close. She asked what I was going to do with my life. I was nineteen, and for some reason people assume by that stage in the game you should have your whole life planned out.

Jen asked me what was next while we were driving in Golden Gate Park. I'm glad she was behind the wheel because I started crying like a crazy person. She was the first friend I told that I was called to be a pastor in The Salvation Army. I was terrified. She loved me and supported me every step of the way, even when I made some stupid choices.

Fast forward five years. Anthony and I finish seminary and our first appointment is back in the San Francisco area. Jen starts coming to my church, and the woman who mentored and loved me now accepted me as her pastor. Crazy, huh?

Anthony and I went through a really rough patch in our marriage, and if things hadn't changed when they did, there is a good chance we wouldn't have made it out. During that rough patch, Jen was there to love us and help support us when it seemed like everything was falling apart and God seemed distant and silent.

Jen has more faith than I've ever seen before. There are too many examples to note, but the latest expression of her faith has come through a diagnosis of leukemia. Jen is sick, and she probably won't be totally healthy again. This cancer might be what takes her to be with Jesus, unless she is hit by a bus or something (she is also one of the clumsiest, accident-prone people I've ever met).

She is still laughing, still loving, still serving Jesus and the hurting in the Bayview district of San Francisco. That place is rough. Jen is just as rough. Jen changes lives every day, and loves like Jesus loves.

Loreen

The last life changer I will write about is my best friend, Loreen Hamilton. Loreen and I couldn't be any different. She is about half my size; not an exaggeration—literally half. We have a different sense of humor (and mine is better; she doesn't appreciate toilet humor nearly as much as she should). She is also way smarter than I am, which I am okay with.

When I first met Loreen, I was in seminary and she came to the school to check it all out. I was her assigned buddy for the weekend. I decided that I didn't like her without giving her much of a chance. (I can be very good at that. Working on it.)

The next year, when she came as a student, things only got worse in my lack of love and care for this girl. We even got to the point where I thought there was a real possibility that I was going to get kicked out of seminary for punching her in the mouth.

Long story short: I didn't punch her, and thus didn't get kicked out. Now we are best friends. Stuff happened in the middle of all that, but most of it I don't remember. At some point, I just began to appreciate her for who she is, someone who isn't like me at all, and we were able to grow a beautiful relationship from that foundation.

Being friends with Loreen has helped me to understand that people change, and grace should be given and received as frequently as possible. Loreen loves me, listens to me, laughs at my gross jokes (sometimes), calls me out on my junk, and is godmother to my kids, and I hers.

Good friends are hard to come by. Even harder when you assume too much and build walls up before giving people a chance. I'm thankful for Loreen, and for the walls she has broken down in my life. (Also, Loreen, pull my finger.)

These life changers have influenced my trajectory through every major step in my life. Because of who they are to me, and what I have been able to recognize in their lives, I am a better person. People who have been rocks in your life often won't mind you standing on their shoulders when you need a better view.

1 Corinthians 11:1 says: *Follow my example, as I follow the example of Christ* (NIV). When we have a history of life changers as a part of our story, we aren't starting from scratch. We aren't trying to figure out everything as if we've never seen it done before. We stand on the shoulders of those who have come before and build on the work they have already done. We stand on their shoulders to use their wisdom and experience to see what is coming. We imitate them as they imitate Christ. Let's stand on the shoulders of those who have come before, as rescuers and examples and friends, to build on who we are, and what we can do for the kingdom.

I am not Lorrie, or the Mortons, or Jen, or Loreen, but if I imitate them as they imitate Christ, I'm off to a great start.

Questions for Reflection:

- Who are/were your life changers?
- Will you commit to letting them know that they have made a difference in your life?
- What will you do to have a positive impact on someone's life this month?
- What are Scriptures that speak about positive influences in our lives?

The Family We Choose

#ILoveHashtags.

I really do love hashtags. They connect people and things that may not otherwise be connected, all via social media. I use them way more than I should.

Here is a short list of the obscure hashtags I use regularly that don't connect anything but me with myself and how funny I think I am:

#**BeautifulBeigeBabies.** Referencing my attractive bi-racial children. Only my own, because if I said that about anyone else's kids, that would be moderately racist.

#**NewBestFriends.** I use this when I meet anyone for the first time (#NotReallyBestFriends).

#**MakesMeLaugh.** So people know I think it's funny, even when I am probably the only one.

#**TeamSouthwest.** For anything about anyone in the Southwest Division of The Salvation Army, USA.

#**IMadeThis.** Be proud of me. I am creative.

#**FamilyYouChoose.** This is my favorite hashtag. I use it when referencing people I have chosen to be my family.

Many people who will read this book come from great families. I hope you thank God for that on the regular. Other than my husband and children, I have no family.

The last time I saw my birth mother was in 2009. The hubs and I went to visit some friends in Portland and decided to go see her. She came down from her apartment stoned out of her mind, calling my five-year-old son terribly racist names. That was the nail in the coffin of our relationship.

Like I said earlier in this book, forgiveness should not be confused with a reconciled relationship. I have forgiven her, but I cannot be in a relationship with her while she continues to make these kinds of choices. It isn't an easy decision, and I wish I could do something else about it. Who knows what the future holds? God isn't done with her yet. I am thankful that God's not done with me either.

You already know that when I was fifteen, I was taken in by the pastors of my church. I am abundantly thankful for what they did for me. Because of them, my whole life changed. I lived in their home; they took care of my basic needs and did the best they could for me. I lived with them for two and a half years, but once I was eighteen, I was gone. I have had a hunger for independence for as long as I can remember.

At times I find myself back where I started. One of the things my birth mother loved to say to me when she was drunk and thought she was hilarious was, "I'm not your mom. I found you on the side of the road in a brown paper bag." On days when I feel especially alone, I picture the me I am now crawling out of an adult-sized brown paper bag on the side of the road, destined to always feel abandoned and thrown away. Not every day feels like that, but there are some days....

I don't have an extended family. But I am beyond thankful for the life changers who filled in the roles I needed, at just the right times (please see the last chapter for a few examples). My whole family is full of people I have chosen. Some may say that that makes me more lucky than most.

In our house we have adopted the custom of having our kids call people we love "Auntie" and "Uncle." One day we were at a big Salvation Army event and my son was with me. As we ran into people we knew I told him, "Say hi to Auntie ___," or "Go give Uncle ___ a high five." After we had done this about ten times, Little Ant asked, "Was that guy my real uncle or fake uncle?" I responded with, "Oh Little, EVERYONE is your fake uncle." He was fine with that clarification.

I really like the story of baby Moses. His mom knew people wanted to kill all the baby boys so she hid him for as long as she could. When she couldn't hide him any longer, she threw him in the river. Ok, maybe "threw him in the river" is a little harsh, but putting your baby in a basket adrift in the Nile is pretty hardcore. Good thing his sister Miriam was there to keep an eye on things.

Miriam was there when Pharaoh's daughter pulled Moses from the water. Maybe she kept him safe along the way. Miriam wasn't his mother, but she stood in the gap for him when he was alone and in need of care.

It was because of Miriam that Moses was able to come back and be safe with his mother until he was weaned. In the ancient world, babies needed their mothers for nutritional support from between two to four years. So Moses was with his mother in safety for an extended period of time because of what Miriam did.

If I could wish something for every young adult, it would be to have Miriams in your lives—solid, intentional mentors. Miriams do things for others that parents should do. You could even have great parents in your life, but maybe you let in a Miriam when your parents seemed distant (even if that is because you pushed your parents away).

I had amazing mentors in my life, and I hope I have been a good mentor to others. People who mentor or intentionally disciple others typically have a healthy and active relationship with the Lord themselves. Others see who they are in Christ and seek them out as mentors. People see what they have and want to live that way too.

Any one of us can be a Miriam. You can take the opportunity to walk along-side people when they feel alone, or when they are struggling to figure things out. Working at camps in the summer provides great opportunities to make these kinds of relationships. You can be with people on staff just a few years younger than you are, and get a chance to show them Jesus in cool ways, and be there as a sounding board on the tough days. (There are a lot of tough days at camp.)

What about the kids who come to youth groups at your church? Younger ones, who have families that let them down, or maybe who just need someone else to talk to, could turn to you for support. You see a kid struggling with homework, help a brotha out. The world doesn't revolve around you or me alone. We are all in this together, and taking the time to intentionally put others first has kingdom impact.

I am a Miriam for one of the most amazing women I've ever met. Her name is Rachel, but most of us call her Rae K (this actually is her real name). Rae K and I met in the summer of 2013. She came to work as a counselor on our Camp Ponderosa Ranch team. She gave out a good first impression, but I'm pretty sure I terrified her. (That happens frequently. Can we add that to my spiritual gift list: has the power to scare the crap outta people upon first interactions?)

Rae K was great that summer, so much so that she became our girls' head counselor the second summer. This job isn't for wimps. She recruited the majority of our staff from her college, and now she was their supervisor. This summer had many high points and several low. But Rae K kept her head in the game the whole time.

She and I talked every day. It was important for her that she maintained the trust of her counselors while being real with me. That's a tough thing to balance. I was the boss—and a pretty scary boss (see the above mentioned spiritual gift). Our relationship grew stronger and the summer ended well. She loves my kids and watches them when we travel. They love Auntie Rae K, which says a lot because our daughter, Hurricane Leilah, usually wears out sitters after one shot.

Rae K lets me into her life in a special way. We laugh, cry, and pray together often. By the time this book is a real published thing, she will be finished with her bachelor's degree in something really smart that I can't ever remember. When she was figuring out what to do next, I filled out references for grad school, the Peace Corps, and a job reference for her to serve the Lord in Hawaii. I'm not sure what will be next for Rae K, but I am thankful that she is receptive to God's leading in her life.

I feel privileged that she would allow me to be a Miriam in her life, and be a part of her journey. She has been a blessing to me more than she knows.

Being in this role in her life helps me stay grounded and focused on what matters most. If we don't make relationships a priority—both with life changers and Miriams—then things can feel empty. When we are struggling to find the motivation to do what is right, or wondering why we shouldn't just give in to that tasty temptation, we can look to the life changers or Miriams as motivation to continue on the right path, instead of living only for ourselves.

As iron sharpens iron, so one person sharpens another (Prov. 27:17 NIV). We need each other. God created us to live in community with him and others. We need people for support just to get through, and we need people to be our strength when we feel like we have none. Like others have done for us, it is important to share the gift of our influence and impact. We need to find ways to be Miriams, to be intentional mentors for those who need a little help or a friend to stand with them along the way.

As we are intentional with these kinds of relationships, we are building the family we choose. That is heaven-on-earth kind of stuff, living out the body of Christ the way it was intended, one Miriam at a time.

Questions for Reflection:

- Who are the people you can be a Miriam to?
- What is the first thing you are gonna do to make that happen?
- Who has been a Miriam in your life? Write this person a letter or email to say thanks.
- What are some Scriptures that talk about mentor relationships?

Serving with Jerks

Jerks are everywhere. Sometimes we think if we leave the church, we will be free from the jerks and people who are difficult to work with. In the church, out of the church, Christian and non-Christian—jerks are everywhere.

Whenever you are around people, you will encounter personalities less than enjoyable to work with. It may not even be because they are jerks; they may just get on your nerves, or be kinda annoying. I hope that I'm not losing my credibility or sanctification by admitting that some people bug.

In every job I've ever had, I've worked with people I would never be best friends with, and some people I would never hang out with if I had the choice. I've been working since I was twelve years old. I was fired from almost every job I had as a teenager because I couldn't handle working with people I didn't like.

My first job was as an optician's assistant. I worked for three dollars an hour, making that paper under the table (also known as working illegally). My main responsibilities were to clean the shop and take apart old glasses for spare parts. I have small scars all over my hands from taking apart those glasses. I cut myself on every pair. My boss never cared that I kept getting hurt, and after awhile she told me that she couldn't even give me any more Band-Aids because it was all becoming too inconvenient.

One day the lady I worked for handed me a shoebox crammed full of hundreds of receipts. This was where she kept all of the things she needed for her taxes. She shoved the box in my face and told me to file them in alphabetical order. I took them to the back office and after the tenth receipt, I was over it. I couldn't see myself singing the alphabet all day, so I decided to come up with a plan B.

My twelve-year-old brain thought it would be a much better idea to just start flushing the receipts down the toilet. That would get me out of this situation much quicker than actually doing the work. (This is one of the many reasons why we shouldn't have twelve-year-olds help with legal tax business.)

I was fired the next day when the toilet backed up and flooded the bathroom with sewage and thousands of dollars worth of reimbursable expense receipts.

Years later I worked at Hot Dog on a Stick. I decided to work there not in spite of the outfits, but because of the outfits. I thought I would look smokin' in those red, yellow, and blue stripes and that tall hat. I pictured the popular guys from my high school walking past and falling in love the minute they saw me stomping lemonade. (Just in case you thought that was a possibility, it never happened.)

In reality I looked like a beach ball, and the girls' uniforms wouldn't even fit. You see, the girls' uniforms have vertical stripes, the boys' horizontal. I rocked those horizontal stripes better than any of those boys.

My manager was one of the meanest people I'd ever met up to that point in my life. He made fat jokes all day, and I often felt left out and made fun of. We also got into an argument once when I saw him making fun of a girl with down's syndrome. He was the worst.

One day he said that we had a mandatory staff meeting at 6 a.m. on a Sunday morning. I told him that he must not fully understand the meaning of the word "mandatory," because there was no way I was going to that. I didn't understand why anyone would go out of the way to attend a meeting for someone who treated all of his employees like they were trash.

I expected several of the other employees to skip out on this meeting because of our mutual distain for the boss. Turns out, I was the only one who didn't go to the meeting; a protest isn't nearly as effective if you are marching alone. I came in Monday afternoon and one of my co-workers said, "Uh, I don't think you have a job here anymore." She was correct.

There were a few other jobs that I got fired from because of disagreements I had with people—sometimes the boss, sometimes other co-workers. These are just the few examples that are funny. The others were not nearly as entertaining for anyone. I didn't get it. I thought that if the people you worked with were rude, you had every right to fight with them, disrespect them, or just quit. That was until I started working for more than just myself.

Once I started to work for the kingdom's sake, everything changed. Sometimes work for the Lord came with a paycheck, like when I worked at camp. Most times it didn't, like when I was doing creative ministry programs with the kids at church as a volunteer. When I saw past myself, I didn't really care who I worked with or for, because it was all for the Lord.

Colossians 3:23-24 says, *Whatever you do, work at it with all your heart, as working for the Lord, not for human masters, since you know that you will receive an inheritance from the Lord as reward. It is the Lord Christ you are serving* (NIV).

Sometimes the "reward" Scripture talks about is something that you won't see until you are in heaven, sitting at the feet of Jesus, having all the cool conversations you've been waiting to have this whole time. Sometimes the "reward" is showing children that they have talents they didn't know about. Or listening to a person who thinks no one cares, but you care—and that changes everything. Or maybe you have to clean a kitchen you didn't mess up, and the reward is providing a meal for people who haven't eaten in days.

In the optician's shop there were jerks, at Hot Dog on a Stick there were jerks, and even in the church as you serve God there will be jerks. But when we are living for more than just ourselves, it doesn't matter. The goal is in sight. Maybe it is kids coming to know Jesus, or building schools in third world countries, or serving coffee and sandwiches to homeless friends on a cold night.

If we see the end game as being the most important thing, so much more than a paycheck, then we can deal with any personality that grinds our gears or rubs us the wrong way. It's not about them, and it's not about you or me. If we are doing things that we really think have kingdom impact, then how stupid and trivial is it to invest emotion or frustration into people or situations that will take away from that eternal significance?

The needs of others, and seizing the opportunity to give a cup of cold water in the name of Jesus, are much more important than us being best friends with everyone we get to work with. I would hope to be so secure in who I am, and my ability to do things for Jesus, that I wouldn't feel the need to only surround myself with people who are my friends, or who think like me, or who act like I do. What a one-sided ministry that would be!

How much more could we do for God if we were operating with as many different types of people as possible. There are people I may think seem cold or distant (and thus think live in the jerk camp), when really they are just super introverted, or have to process and think about things differently than I do. Or maybe they just see the world very differently than I do.

In Scripture we see that Jesus surrounded himself with a diverse group of people in the disciples. Two of the twelve were polar opposites. In Matthew 9:9, Jesus calls Matthew, the tax collector, to be one of his disciples. I like reading this passage from *The Living Bible*. It says that Matthew *jumped up and went along with him*. No hesitation. No second thoughts. Matthew was a dude who was despised. He was a traitor, a robber, a social outcast, a public enemy. He worked for the Roman government to take money from his own people. When he was called, there was a special point made to mention his job description, a definition of how vile he was and how much he was hated. The popular opinion of the day was that tax collectors were so bad, they were cut off from God. Jesus knew everything that Matthew had done and all he had become and still said, "I want you to come with me."

The dude who was the polar opposite of Matthew was Simon, the Zealot. "The Zealots" were a political party who wanted to overthrow the Roman government. They were even known to kill their fellow Jews who wanted to negotiate with Rome. Simon, the Zealot, joined Team Jesus, and who else was on the team? Matthew, the tax collector. Matthew sold himself out to the Roman government.

These men were exact opposites. They had every reason to hate each other, but instead they shared meals together. They shared a life of service together. They may not have seen eye to eye. But it's like Simon gets to the first huddle of Team Jesus and when he sees Matthew sitting across the table he thinks, *Ok, this guy and I are going to change the world together.*

So maybe, just maybe, that person who drives you insane is in your life for a reason. What if that person is a gift from the Lord to teach you something? Don't expect me to know what that is! I'm not God and I'm not in your head. But I do know that everyone is good for something, even if sometimes they are just a good reminder of what not to do.

As I go through my mental Rolodex of memories I have of when people were less than kind (for those of you who were born after 1989, this is what people used to use to hold those outdated slips of paper called business cards)—stories of when people showed their humanness much more than they showed the love of Christ—I am thankful I have all of these examples of what not to do. How not to treat people. How not to live. How not to make people feel small and belittled.

God isn't finished with any of us yet. Just because someone was a jerk doesn't mean he is destined to live that way forever. Let's say the person we are talking about really is a jerk, not just someone who is very different from you. Let's say that this person really is mean and snarly, always making other people feel like old garbage. If a person constantly treats others like this, there has to be a reason why. We have to ask what is going on in people's hearts if their claws are always out.

If you have a Grinch in your Whoville, maybe all that person needs is to be exposed to folks who know the genuine love of Christ, even when the Grinch strikes out in hurt or anger. Instead of giving up on the Grinches and jerks, let's commit to loving and serving them, too. Let's pray for the softening of hearts for them. (And us. Serving with jerks isn't for wimps.)

Maybe an extra measure of love and grace will be enough over time to rehydrate even the most shriveled hearts. Maybe you showing Jesus even on the tough days will motivate them to restore their relationships with God, and turn the corner on the way they treat others. Even if the way we live and love changes nothing, we can't ever stop being who we are called to be. Misery loves company, and hard hearts are contagious.

My mantra when working with people who are difficult is: I will do whatever I can to not become what I dislike most about them. If someone gossips about us, our first response is to gossip about them. If someone is short or rude with us, we are rude right back. When we get sucked into this, we become a jerk, too.

I don't ever wanna be that dude. I don't ever want to be the person that others feel they can't work with, or serve alongside. I know I've been guilty of this in the past, but I hope to never be that person again.

Only love.

Only grace.

Only forgiveness.

Only compassion.

Only kindness.

Only Jesus.

No matter what.

Questions for Reflection:

- Have you ever had to work with someone who was difficult, or operated very differently than you do?
- How did you show Jesus in this situation, or how do you wish you would have shown Jesus?
- What are some Scripture passages on showing love?
- What is your plan next time you get to work with or be around someone who is difficult?

Note: The comparison between Matthew and Simon was taken from a podcast by Craig Bowler. Not my original thoughts, but they were too brilliant not to share.

The Dating Test

When I was a teenager, I was mentored by a brilliant woman; I've talked about her a bit already—Jen. She got on my case when I needed someone to call me out on my stuff, and she let me ugly-cry on her shoulder when I needed that too. (I needed that more times than I'd like to share at this point, so please stop being so nosey and mind your business.)

One day I was telling her about a guy I thought was real fine at the time. This was not a good dude—not good for me, and not really good for anyone. Instead of telling me I needed to direct my attention elsewhere (which we all know makes girls run faster toward the dummy they are chasing after), she gave me this five question quiz to evaluate if the person that I was crushing on was someone I should consider dating. I have changed it up a little since then. I just wanted to give credit that this is not my original idea.

Here's how this works: have a person in mind when you ask yourself these questions. Each answer is a score of one to ten; one is as bad as it gets and ten is a-may-zing. Then you take the total score and average it out to a letter grade. I hope that you aren't so repelled by math or numbers that you skip this part. This is where it gets tricky, and would be different from person to person. For me, I say that you could date someone who scores a C+ or B- on the test. I don't know if it is fair to expect people to score 100% straight away. Where you stand on this part is on you.

When I first met Anthony, he was not an A, mostly because he didn't have an active relationship with Jesus. Friends, please don't hear me say that it is ideal to date non-Christians. It worked out for me, and he got reacquainted with the Lord soon after we started dating, but that's not always the case. Most times it seems like the Jesus followers get pulled away from their values and change their worldviews instead of the non-Christians turning to Jesus. Just a heads up about that.

Everything else on the dating test he excelled in. He was smokin' hot, and still is. I could definitely handle looking at that man every day for the rest of my life. I knew he would be a great dad because he helped raise his siblings and cared deeply for his family. He loved and invested in my little brother from the start, which showed me a lot about his character. He was a sergeant at the sheriff's department—good job, making money and handling his business. We shouldn't chase people because of money, but if they can't take care of themselves, they will never be our equals in marriage. If they can't keep a job now, there is a good chance they won't ever be able to keep a job. Like I said before, he didn't love Jesus, but he acted like Jesus more than anyone else I knew. Anthony genuinely loves others and puts people before himself. He is a great listener and wants to do everything he can to make the world a better place.

People grow and change together, but it isn't fair or realistic to expect that you can change someone into the person you'd like them to be. The best relationships happen when people value each other and are realistic about who they really are and what they bring to the table, and are excited and open to growing and changing together. What you see is what you get. You can't expect that a characteristic, annoying habit or major flaw will ever change. Be honest about what the issue is, keep talking about it, and go from there. But if it is a deal breaker, you may need to move on, even if you've invested a ton of time. It's better to figure that out now than years down the road when careers and kids are involved.

The person you will eventually marry is obviously someone you've dated, and he or she will have already passed the dating test to end up in that pool. That is why, when it comes to getting married, the person needs to score an A on the dating test. This is going to be the person that you are with every day for the rest of your life until one of you dies. Don't settle for less than God's best.

Here are the five questions:

1. **How attracted to the person are you?**
   Looks will fade, but they are important. You are going to wake-up next to that person every day; you should like what you see.

2. **What kind of parent will this person be?**
   You can often tell this by the way the person treats others who are of no personal consequence, or the way the person acts towards small kids when not trying to impress you.

3. **How is this person at accomplishing goals, paying bills, and the overall handling of business?**
   Most people want to date and eventually get married to someone who will be an equal partner in their lives, not someone that they are going to have to parent or tell what to do all the time.

4. **How much does this person love Jesus?**
   As Christians, we want to be with people who have the same foundation in life that we do. If they don't love Jesus with their whole hearts, then their decision-making processes and values will always be different than someone who does.

5. Does this person act like Jesus?

People can say they love Jesus, and go to church on the regu-lar, but if they don't act like Jesus, what is it all for? We should want to be with someone real, and if a person is claiming to be a Christian, then that person should be actively trying to live like Jesus.

To be the kind of person who an A wants to be with, you need to be an A also. Are you the kind of person who takes care of yourself and handles your business? Do you treat people with respect and kindness? Do you love others even if they have nothing to offer you in return? How much do you really love Jesus, and is that love reflected in your day-to-day actions? What are you doing to constantly better your-self—not just so you can find a boyfriend/girlfriend, who could eventually become a spouse, but so you can be the best you can be for yourself and for your service for Jesus.

When I met my husband, I put him to this dating test, and on June 5, 2004, we got hitched. Things in our relationship haven't always been easy, but when you marry the right person for the right reasons, marriage can be bliss—a place where both lives are made better, and God is glorified through it all.

Questions for Reflection:

- What does the Bible say about marriage?
- Do you want to get married one day (if you aren't already)? Why or why not?
- If you are in a relationship, do some evaluating using the dating test. Did you learn any-thing new?
- Do some self-evaluation using the dating test. Is there anything that you need to modify to be the best you possible?

Love and Sex Are Not Synonyms

In the last chapter we talked about how to decide if someone we are crushing on is worth dating. You have someone in your sights. You like this person, and the person likes you too. Before I was married, I felt like this never happened. It was a unicorn; we talk about it and hope to see it one day, but seems like it may remain a myth forever. I had lots of crushes. If you were tall, I crushed. If you were a musician, I crushed. If you had stretched ears, I crushed. If you had a puppy with you, I crushed. If you smiled at me, even on accident, I crushed. You may call that being boy-crazy; I call it being non-discriminatory. But the vast majority of dudes I had a crush on had no interest in me at all.

So when there was a guy I liked who liked me too, the butterflies in my gut felt more like polyphemus moths. (Those are giant moths with a six-inch wingspan; totally harmless, but super creepy. Google it). The feelings of like, to like-like, to love seemed out of control sometimes. If you like someone and that person likes you, things can go from zero to naked in no time. I'm not saying that it's a good idea, but it's not difficult to understand how things can get there.

Maybe you like the person more than the person likes you, so you start to think that if you go further physically, that person will like you more. I hope that our sense of self-worth and self-esteem is high enough to know that we are worth more than that. We are worth more than throwing our bodies at people in the hopes that our physical actions will make us loveable. Even if that "works"—if the person likes you more because of what you do for him or her physically—then that is probably not the kind of person you really want to be with.

I won't judge you for making some wrong choices in the people you have dated. Talk about the pot calling the kettle stupid for getting involved with dirt bags ... or however that saying goes. I've done my fair share of that.

There was one guy I liked when I was finishing high school and for a couple years after. I liked this guy a lot. Like, it was a problem. I didn't think about anything else. I became the kind of person I thought he would like: my favorite color changed, the kind of music I liked changed, and my standards across the board fell apart. The worst part is that he was clear that he wasn't that into me, but I'm about solutions, so I thought I could change that. I lost weight, mostly through my eating disorder. I replaced my glasses with contacts. I went into debt buying cool clothes I couldn't afford. I did everything I could think of to make him notice me, and it worked.

I hadn't seen him in a few weeks because we lived about forty-five minutes apart. I went to his work to say hi. We chatted for a little bit and made plans to see each other later. As I was walking out he said to me, "Lisa, you look really good. You're almost pretty now." Almost. Not pretty yet. Not good enough yet. But almost. Here is where I let you in on how insecure I was: I was excited by what he said. I thought, *You're almost there, Lisa. Just a little further and you will be good enough.* If someone said that to me now, there is a good chance I would at least daydream of punching him in the mouth.

I am so thankful that things didn't work out with me and that guy. One of the things that happens when you get old and wise is you become thankful for un-answered prayers. Praise God that he knew so much better than I did. Just a few months after things fell apart with me and this guy, the guy who never liked me anyway, I met Anthony.

I was working in customer service at Bed, Bath and Beyond in Salinas, California, and Anthony came in to buy some picture frames. He started talking to one of the other girls who worked there, and I noticed that she was flirting with him. I thought he was handsome and I didn't like her, so I sent her to the back of the store to get his frames. I sent this girl to the wrong part of the store intentionally so she would be back there for awhile. As soon as she was gone, I swooped in.

While she was searching we talked and flirted. I thought, *This guy is handsome. He's brown, and that might piss off my adopted parents, which would be cool.* (I had just turned 20. Doing things to upset older folks still had a lot of appeal.) *He also looks like a thug, and I've never dated a thug before.* (Turns out he wasn't a thug; he was a cop.)

The girl I sent to get his frames was heading back up to the front of the store, wearing her "I hate Lisa for sending me on a treasure hunt in all the wrong places" face. I knew that our time was going to be up soon, and because I am a strong, asser-tive woman, I took a business card, wrote my name and number on the back, and slid it across the counter—before he asked for it. Ladies, if you see something you want, don't be afraid to go for it. Dudes like that kind of confidence.

I said to him, "I don't normally do this, but if you would like to call me...." Then my brain shut off. I just kept saying, "You could call me. If you wanna call me. Then you could call me. And after you call me, you can call me." So much for great confidence and assertiveness....

Despite my blundering attempts, he took the business card and called me two days later. We dated and fell in love. I found my unicorn. I liked him and he liked me back. I invited him to church. He came, fell in love with the Lord, and was fully embraced by the body of Christ.

I was honest about everything, more honest than I'd ever been with anyone. I told him that I was sold out for Jesus, and I wouldn't be having sex again until I was married. He accepted that and was always respectful of those boundaries. Then my boundaries got weaker and less visible. What started out as a resolve of steel became a puddle of suggestions. We were in love and it seemed normal to get physical. Everyone I knew was intimate with their boyfriends or girlfriends.

We got pregnant.

My life fell apart. I felt like a liar and a fraud. The news got out and the scarlet letter was painted. Everywhere I went I heard things like, "We never thought it would be you, Lisa." I was in church one day, crying my eyes out, huge tears full of shame and embarrassment. This old woman, a pillar in the church, came up to me and started rubbing my back. I thought she was there to console me, but instead, as she rubbed my back she said, "I know you are sad. We are all sad, too. We [speaking for the entire church body] thought you really could have been somebody. Now, who knows what you will do. It's all too bad." In my mind this was what the world thought of me. Jesus became a silent stranger as I embraced the labels and stares of disappointment as things that I earned and I deserved.

We got married when we were three months pregnant, not because we were pregnant, but because we loved each other. That's an important distinction.

Our story turned out better than most whose relationships started the way ours did. The odds weren't in our favor, but I am thankful that God is in the business of taking our mistakes and turning them into beautiful things. Beautiful things like my son, who shows me Jesus at every opportunity. Who teaches us about faith and love and seeking after God's heart in all we do. That boy is one of the greatest gifts I've ever received.

I thought love and sex were interchangeable words. Sex and love are not synonyms. They don't mean the same thing, and just because you feel like you are in love, that doesn't mean that sex in any form needs to be included in the equation. Not just because you could get knocked up, but because when you are intimate with someone, you give that person a piece of your innermost being. When you give your body, your heart cannot be excluded.

God created us to be intimate with the person to whom we are married and committed to spending the rest of our lives with. Having sex strengthens the bonds of marriage, and when it happens the way God intended, it is a beautiful thing. Sex is great, not something to be feared, but something to look forward to within marriage. When we have get-downs with people we aren't married to, it becomes very confusing. Our hearts and minds get tangled up in something that will never make sense.

I don't want to talk about this as the giant wagging finger telling you to abstain from sex just because God said so. (He did and that is enough, but there is more.)

Our hearts just can't handle it. That's not how we are wired or how we were created. This is especially true if we are having sex to fill a void we have in our hearts.

When I was a teenager and lost my virginity, I just wanted someone to care about me. I wanted someone to tell me I was worth loving, and I thought sex was an expression of love. I couldn't have been more wrong. Having sex to feel loved resulted in the opposite effect. I felt more discarded and used than ever before.

I wanted a whole heart. Those empty places couldn't be filled by sex or drinking or any of the other things we do to feel fulfilled. The only way we can feel whole and restored is by accepting the love and grace of Jesus, and walking in his light instead of being controlled by our own feelings or selfishness.

When I first met Jesus, I sought after a whole heart. As I grow closer in my relationship with the Creator, I seek a holy heart. I want what Jesus wants. I want to love like Jesus loves. I want to show kindness and acceptance the way Jesus does.

The hole in my heart led to me finding a whole heart, and continues to mature in my holy heart.

Questions for Reflection:

- If you have been intimate outside of marriage, take some time in prayer to talk to Jesus about it. Have a tough conversation and be honest about why you went there, and seek out the restoration and healing that only Jesus offers.
- What are some Scriptures about sex? Look at how it is beautiful, but can also be destructive. Song of Solomon has some great stuff about married sex being wonderful.
- If you have someone in your life now who you are physical with, what are things you need to do to set up healthy boundaries?
- Take some time to accept the grace and forgiveness that Jesus is waiting to give you, no matter what the reason.

Crushing Expectations

Standards. Rules. Morals. Expectations. Limitations. Boundaries. Values.

We have so much placed on us as young Christians, the weight of it can feel crushing. Here is what Christians are supposed to look like, or sound like, or wear, or listen to, or say. Here are the only appropriate jokes to laugh at. Here are the right people to hang out with. Please watch only these movies, and only with people of the same gender. Don't go there, or be that, or listen to them. And do it all with a smile.

Sometimes the expectations of others can be too much to handle. The standards placed on us that are based on the personal opinions of others instead of the instructions of Jesus can push us away instead of drawing us closer to Christ.

When I was a teenager, I had pretty regular interactions with this old lady at my church. She said that she loved Jesus, but based on her actions I would say that was debatable. Loving Jesus = loving others. If you have no love for others then ... you know what I am saying.

Anyway, this lady was probably about 300 years old and she was snarly. Only mean things came out of her mouth. One day I overheard her say, "Only whores wear red nail polish." I went out that night and found the brightest, most obnoxious red polish ninety-nine cents could buy. It was my new favorite thing. I made sure to put on a fresh coat whenever I knew I would see this lady at the church. (She didn't love it nearly as much as I did.)

Caveat: instigating fights with old folks doesn't show the love of Jesus. If they already have hard hearts and don't seem like they know Jesus, you may be pushing them closer to hell sooner than they might get there on their own.

It just really bugged me that she felt so strongly about her personal opinions, opinions that seemed so backwards. They had nothing to do with the kingdom, and were more distractive and divisive than anything else. Her views on such things really didn't matter. But there are standards that do matter.

God wants to restore us. He wants us to grow and blossom into the people he created us to be. That means that we don't get to stay the people we started out as. I'm talking about the stuff that matters. Eternal things. Kingdom things. Kindness things. Holy living things. Not the color of your nail polish or hair, if you wear the right clothes or have perfected the Christian mask you think you need to wear. Those things are stupid, and worrying about them wastes God's time.

My hubs says something that I really like. Well, he says a few things I really like, but right now I'm just talking about one specific thing. "It's our responsibility to show Jesus to others, so that when he knocks on the door of their hearts, he won't be a stranger, because they have seen Jesus first in us."

It is important that we show Jesus in the things that matter because people are watching us. They are watching, not to catch us getting it wrong, but they are watching waiting for us to get it right so they can see how it's done. How are Christians supposed to act? How are they supposed to treat others? How do they find joy in a world full of crap and sadness? What's their motivation? If people are seeking the answers to these questions, and they know that you and I love Jesus, they will watch us to see how we do it, so they can figure out how to do it themselves, or if it's even worth doing at all.

When I got knocked up with my son, I was scared out of my mind. I had no idea how to be a mom. What are moms supposed to do all day? How do they interact with their kids? What are the right things to say or the wrong things to say? I was lost and had no idea. One day I made a list of the things I wanted to do as a mother, and one of those things was taking my kid to the park.

I had no idea what you are supposed to do with a kid at the park. I'd never been to a park with my mom. I took a notepad and a pen and waddled my pregnant self to the park. I sat on a bench and watched parents and their kids—that's right, like a crazy stalker—and took notes. Here were my in-depth scientific conclusions:

- Push kid on swing until he gets over it. This may take awhile.
- Play in sandbox. Check for cat turds first. Bring sand toys to reduce sand throwing and eating.
- Bring snacks to reduce tantrums and crying; then make sure you have enough for the kid, too.
- Have hand sanitizer; this place is disgusting.

There will be times when we don't have the answers for things. We watch others who do to help us figure it out. Often the dudes you're watching have no idea that they are case studies in how to get it right. There have been times, and there will be more times, when YOU are that dude. People are watching, and you get to show them Jesus, even if you don't know it.

This may sound like a lot of pressure, and there is a lot that can hang in the balance. But no one expects you and I to get it perfect all the time. They just want to know how to get started and if it is even worth trying. Jesus gave us great examples of what this looks like.

- The bleeding woman in Mark 5. She thought if she only touched the edge of his clothes she would be healed. Faith is simple.

- The temptation Jesus faced from Satan in Matthew 4. Jesus told him to kick rocks and it was over. Temptation is beatable.
- Friends lowered their paralyzed buddy through a roof to be healed by Jesus in Luke 5. We all need homies who are willing to go the extra mile. Friends are important.
- The commands to love people who are jerks from Luke 6. People who are impolite, insulting, and intrusive need Jesus too. Kindness is hard.

As humans, it's part of our nature to complicate things, to add more rules or standards than are really necessary for an active life with Jesus. The Pharisees were really good at this. I'm not saying you can do whatever you want, free from repercussions and consequences. What I am saying is that it is important to live it if we say we believe it, for our sake and for the sake of those who are watching, just trying to figure it out along with us.

Like I said, people want to know if it is even worth trying.

Being a Christian doesn't mean that from the moment you accept Jesus into your life, everything is going to be chocolate hearts and rainbow farts. Life is still hard and bad things still happen. But as Christians—as little Christs—things have to be different for us. That difference is hope. Hope that there is a reason for all of this. Hope that tomorrow will be better than today. Hope that our families or friends who hate us or make fun of us for loving Jesus will someday change their minds. Hope that things will get better. Hope that our future will be bright. Hope that we will leave a legacy that glorifies God and makes a difference. HOPE.

The people who are watching us need to know that being a Christian is worth it. People want to be assured that this isn't just a social club that only lets certain people in and prides itself on all of the things we abstain from. *Look at all the things we don't do!* We have the creator of the universe in our corner, and that's the best we can come up with? Lame. I wouldn't want to be a part of that. There has to be more.

Being a Christian isn't easy, but the good outweighs the bad every day. Even on the worst days, when we feel defeated from all angles, we have hope that God knows what's going on, and he has not given up on us. We have the hope that Jesus is a part of all of this and is on our side. We have the assurance that the Holy Spirit (who is just as important as God and Jesus in the Trinity, but is so often forgotten) is our comforter and is alongside us for every part of the journey—especially the crap days.

We can live this hope as an example of why any of this friggen matters. There are people who have no hope and are searching for it in all the wrong places. We have an opportunity to show them that things can be different, because we are different. Not because of the restrictions and expectations that people's opinions place on us, but because of the hope and guidance that Jesus gives as we grow in our relationship with him and spend time in the Word. We show them this when our actions and our words are same-same, when we put the masks down and really live like Jesus.

Questions for Reflection:

- How would your life be different if you were living out the hope we have in Jesus every day?
- What are some Scriptures that talk about Jesus' expectations?
- What are some expectations or rules that people have placed on you that seem unrealistic?
- What do you think God expects of you?
- What do you expect of yourself?
- Who is watching and learning from your example?

Foot-Phobic

I hate feet with my whole heart. I'm grossed out by them, and avoid them at all costs. I don't think there is anything redeeming about feet. I mean, I am thankful that God created us with them, because it would be much more difficult to get around if our legs ended with stumps on our ankles. But other than the practicality of us using feet to move, they are disgusting things. They are ugly and smelly and require a ton of maintenance and money (because even though they gross me out, you better believe my toes will always be painted and I will have cute shoes; double standards I guess).

Once when I was working at camp as a teenager, I spent a break day with a car full of people. A friend was driving, I was in the passenger seat and there were three other friends in the back. The person who was in the back middle seat decided it would be hilarious to play a disgusting and friendship-altering joke on me. She took her sandal off and steadily held her black-bottomed, camp-dirt-encrusted foot inches from my face. I was looking forward and didn't see this unfold. I just heard someone from the back say, "Hey, Lisa."

Her foot smashed into my left cheek as I turned my head. It took me a second to figure out what it was. Never had I experienced a foot so close to my face. I just knew it was cold and slightly wet as it touched my cheek. I sat back to evaluate the situation, and when I realized what had happened, I had the freak-out of the century.

I started screaming, and couldn't stop. My flight response was in high gear. I started clawing at the car window as if it were a plywood coffin and I was being buried alive. I also may or may not have tried to jump out of a moving vehicle to escape my tormentors.

This was a traumatizing experience (only for me, everyone else was pee-your-pants laughing), and I'm a little upset with you for bringing it up. When I say that I hate feet, I hope you understand how far this extends in my life. So when Scripture says anything about feet, it weirds me out and makes me feel uncomfortable, like when Mary Magdalene anointed Jesus with expensive perfume. This is one of those stories that appears in all four gospels. The one from Luke is my favorite. Luke 7:36-48 says this:

> *When one of the Pharisees invited Jesus to have dinner with him, he went to the Pharisee's house and reclined at the table. A woman in that town who*

lived a sinful life learned that Jesus was eating at the Pharisee's house, so she came there with an alabaster jar of perfume. As she stood behind him at his feet weeping, she began to wet his feet with her tears. Then she wiped them with her hair, kissed them and poured perfume on them.

When the Pharisee who had invited him saw this, he said to himself, "If this man were a prophet, he would know who is touching him and what kind of woman she is—that she is a sinner."

Jesus answered him, "Simon, I have something to tell you."

"Tell me, teacher," he said.

"Two people owed money to a certain moneylender. One owed him five hundred denarii, and the other fifty. Neither of them had the money to pay him back, so he forgave the debts of both. Now which of them will love him more?"

Simon replied, "I suppose the one who had the bigger debt forgiven."

"You have judged correctly," Jesus said.

Then he turned toward the woman and said to Simon, "Do you see this woman? I came into your house. You did not give me any water for my feet, but she wet my feet with her tears and wiped them with her hair. You did not give me a kiss, but this woman, from the time I entered, has not stopped kissing my feet. You did not put oil on my head, but she has poured perfume on my feet. Therefore, I tell you, her many sins have been forgiven—as her great love has shown. But whoever has been forgiven little loves little."

Then Jesus said to her, "Your sins are forgiven" (NIV).

So this chick had some guts. She had a bad reputation. Popular opinion is that she was a prostitute. *The Message* calls her the "town harlot." I think that those assumptions may be a little far-fetched. But whatever her deal was, she had been through some crap and probably made a few bad choices.

She knew that she had screwed up her life, and she knew who Jesus really was. She had a lot to be sorry for, and lots of reasons to be thankful for the saving grace of the Messiah. Mary went and bought some expensive perfume, so expensive that it would have cost a year's wages, approximately 300 denarii. Most day laborers earned one denarius a day. That would currently be the equivalent of a person who works full-time earning minimum wage going out and buying a bottle of perfume that costs about $20,000 and pouring it on Jesus' feet.

It wasn't about the cost of the perfume. It was about recognizing who Jesus was, and that his grace was worth more than we could ever offer in return. Like I said before, I have a huge issue with feet, but historically speaking people didn't have the same issues with feet then as a lot of us (I know I'm not the only one) do now.

When we lived in San Francisco, I met a woman named Minerva (not her real name). She was a server at a restaurant close by our church building. When she waited on us, I noticed that she was pregnant ... well, *I thought* I noticed she was pregnant. It's one of those things, you want to say something because it's a great conversation starter, but there is that possibility that she's not knocked up—maybe she's just chubby or had a big lunch. I took the risk anyway and asked if she was pregnant. She thankfully said yes and told me she was almost halfway through the pregnancy. She also had two other kids, ten and seven years old.

I told her what we did, and how close The Salvation Army was. We had youth programs on Wednesday and I offered to pick her kids up if she would like. I gave her my card and she called me the next day asking for a ride for her kids. This started a great relationship between Minerva and me. Her kids came to everything and in time she did too; the three of them were coming regularly and I even got to dedicate her third baby once he was born.

Minerva wasn't married, but was living with the baby daddy, and he wasn't a good dude. I was suspicious of some domestic violence but wasn't sure. I was taking her home after church one day when she dropped a bomb: her baby was just over a month old and she was pregnant again.

This would be surprising for most people, but it was a bomb for me because my marriage was being destroyed due to our infertility struggles. We had been trying to get pregnant for over two years at this point and it was ripping us apart. Then this woman comes into my life with no regard for doing things God's way, and she gets to have babies as often as some people clean their bathrooms or change their bed sheets. The jealousy was infuriating, and the judgment was maddening.

Why couldn't I have that? I was married and stable and serving God, and all we wanted was another child and a sibling for our son. I felt bitter and angry toward both Minerva and God. I was sure I was being punished for not doing it right the first time. God became an angry, vengeful God who I thought was laughing at our misfortune and unhappiness. In my imagination he was shaking his giant finger in the sky telling us, "That's what you get. Better luck next time." Things were rapidly declining in my marriage and in my faith.

About a month after we found out Minerva was pregnant with number four, I got a call from her at 7 a.m. Her boyfriend had pushed her down the stairs and she lost the baby. She had spent the night in the ER and had just been released. She asked if I would pray for her. I did. I felt like all I could do was pray for her. Minerva and I had a common enemy. We could both be mad at God together.

Just a few days later, Minerva called me again and told me she was going to need to have a procedure called a DNC. This is where doctors go in and make sure there are no bits of life left behind. She asked if I would give her a ride because she was going to be under anesthesia and her boyfriend, who caused this horrible thing to happen, refused to take her to the hospital. Classy guy, huh?

We got to the hospital and she got all ready for the procedure, dressed in the ambiguous blue gown and cap that makes everyone look marvelous, and she started to panic. She told the doctors that she wouldn't go under anesthesia unless I could stay with her the whole time. After some arguing, and some screaming from Minerva, the doctors agreed. I put on the same fetching blue gown and cap as Minerva wore. We were the same. Two women, hurting and broken, in the same space, holding hands. We held on tight as things got started. Once the anesthesia kicked in, her grip turned into something more like the hand of a sleeping child. I held on tight to Minerva. I felt like I owed her that much.

I stood there holding her as I promised I would during this intense procedure and I thought, as tears streamed down my face and onto the blue gown, *Who am I? Who am I to stand in the gap for this woman and do what Jesus would do if he were here, something simple but profound. Something that Jesus would do even if it made him uncomfortable or sad. When I signed up to be a pastor, I never expected to be here, mourning this loss of life due to violence as I stand here infertile and broken. God, who am I? And why me?*

Sometimes God will ask us to do things that make us feel uncomfortable. For real uncomfortable, not just I-don't-really-like-feet-so-when-my-church-does-a-foot-washing-ceremony-I-will-hide-in-the-bathroom kind of uncomfortable. When I stood in that operating room with Minerva, I felt uneasy. That scenario wasn't in my mental picture of what my life and ministry was going to look like.

Sometimes we get so afraid of the unknown or the uncomfortable that we exclude Jesus from the equation. We keep the expensive perfume to ourselves, or we don't interact with the person who is homeless or struggling with addiction. The pregnant teen who was raped and is scared will make you feel uncomfortable. Situations where kids get abused by their parents will make you feel uncomfortable. Ministry is messy, and things can get ugly.

Are we willing to do anything for Jesus? Does ministry or service have to look a certain way for us to be willing to do it? Or are we willing to take all we have and dump it at the feet of Jesus? Not just begrudgingly willing, but *eagerly* willing to love and serve those in the margins who may make us feel uncomfortable or angry or bitter or jealous or sad? Are we ready to do absolutely anything to show the love of Jesus?

We all have things in our lives we would rather not do. Maybe if you were sexually assaulted, talking with someone who has had this same pain will be extra difficult for you to handle. Maybe if you were abused by a parent or sibling, serving someone who has been in a similar situation will take you to a tough place emotionally. We all have our stuff, and some things are harder for us to deal with than others. Are we willing to stand in that place of pain or shame with the one who is hurting, point to the light above the pit and say, "Things are better when we are up there. Let me give you a boost out of this pit. I've been here before and I know what it's like. Let's climb out together"

Serving others in the name of Jesus isn't for wimps. Are you up for the challenge and hurt that comes along with it all? Or are you too foot-phobic, too afraid of the uncomfortable things to really be the hands of Jesus and do his work, no matter what?

Questions for Reflection:

- What ministry situations make you the most uncomfortable?
- What are some Scriptures that talk about less-than-glamorous or popular things?
- Is there anything that you would absolutely not do in your service for Jesus?
- What's your plan to get ready to do anything for God?

Nobody's Puppet

Are you a Christian because you made the personal decision to follow Jesus with all you are and all you have? Or are you a Christian because your parents are Christians, and you were raised in a Christian home? Are you a servant for Jesus because you can't imagine doing anything else and feeling fulfilled? Or are you a servant for Jesus because that is the family business? *Everyone else works for God and the kingdom, so I guess I will too....*

There are people who have grown up in Christian homes their whole lives. What a great thing that must be. I may or may not be slightly jealous of lives like that. If that is you, please don't see that blessing for anything less than it is. But if all you have ever known is a life and home filled with Jesus, you may need to do some introspective searching to make sure that the Jesus you know is an up-close-and-personal Jesus, not just a stranger who lives in your home.

Many people come to know Christ though a crisis or crazy choices. These people's conversion stories are often very big and dramatic. They know exactly how and when they met Jesus. They know who they were before Christ, and will do whatever they can to never go back to that dark and desperate place. But what if that isn't you? What if you accepted Jesus as a child, and did your best to live the way we try to teach kids to live? What if you never touched drugs or alcohol, or got caught up in the wrong crowd?

Is Jesus still the savior of your life even if he's never had to pull you out of a slimy pit of sin and shame? Does Jesus still have the throne of your heart even if you've never had to push any idols off to offer him a seat? This can be harder to recognize if you haven't had a major conversion-via-crisis experience. Even if your life wasn't filled with catastrophes, your relationship with God and your conversion can be just as real, and the story of your life can be just as powerful as anyone else's. Own your story, and rejoice in the saving grace of Jesus, whatever that's looked like in your world.

I don't really know that there is a specific prayer or certain words that we need to say for God to hear us, or that Jesus is ever like, "Oh, you gotta say the magic words if you want me to live in your heart." I think the prayer of salvation is important: admitting that we are sinners in need of a Savior, and that Savior is Jesus. We can't do it on our own, and we need him by our side every day to help us do the best we can with what we have. But I don't think there are specific words that we need to use to seal the salvation deal, ya dig?

If you can't remember ever having a legit conversation with Jesus, asking him to guide your steps and be a part of it all, then today is as good a day as ever. Here is something that I like to say when I have the crazy-amazing privilege of leading people to the feet of Jesus for the first time. Again, none of these are magic, must-say-to-get-the-golden-ticket words. I'm pretty sure God cares more about the state of your heart than the minutiae of your words. But if you are trying to figure out what this looks like, here is a good place to start:

Hey God (I start almost all my prayers out this way). I come to you thankful that you hear us all the time. I am asking for forgiveness for the things that I've done that have separated me from you. I'm a sinner, and I need the help of Jesus to be the me you created me to be.

I believe Jesus died for my sins so I don't have to be held captive by guilt or shame anymore. I wanna be different. I want to make better choices, to live a life that is closer to Christ. I want to turn away from the things that have held me prisoner and dance in the freedom that Jesus brings.

Jesus, I give you the main seat in my life. I believe that you rose from the dead and have the power to do anything. I ask you to be my Savior, Lord of my life, and be with me and guide me every step of the way.

Thanks for loving me, Jesus. Thanks in advance for transforming my life.

Amen.

So if you don't know for sure that you fully belong to Jesus, then this is the first step: admitting that you need help and Jesus is it. It's important that your faith in Jesus is real, that it belongs to you, and that you aren't just regurgitating your family's faith, your church's faith, or repeating the Christian-y sounding things that you've heard your whole life.

So you know who Jesus is. You guys are homies. He has the throne of your heart. At this point my question is: Why do you believe the things you believe? I ask because often when we grow up in the church, we believe the things we've been told to believe, or the things that we've heard over and over. We may not have ever read them in Scripture for ourselves, and they might not even be accurate.

Before we went to seminary, I helped lead worship on Sunday mornings. There were a ton of times when I used the verse, *"For where two or three gather in my name, there am I with them"* (Matt. 18:20 NIV). I heard lots of people use this phrase in regards to worship and just thought that it was one of the typical things that worship leaders said, so I said it too. I hadn't really studied the Bible in depth before, and when I did, my mind was blown in several areas. This was one of them.

This verse has NOTHING to do with people coming together in worship. Really, when we think that it does, it makes God a small god. He isn't present unless two or three are together? What happens to my prayers when I'm alone? They just get ignored or what? This verse is all about reconciliation. When people are fighting, but decide to come together and seek reconciliation, God is present in that. Nothing about worship. All about the body of Christ setting aside selfishness and pride to be a community of believers who are more focused on Jesus than we are on ourselves.

I believed what I had heard, and it wasn't even true. My faith was thrown for a loop. I started thinking, *What else do I believe that I'm wrong about?* I decided that I was going to question the things that I'd heard and not yet read for myself.

I'm not saying that we shouldn't believe or trust our leaders or those who guide us, but we should be able to read and think about it all for ourselves, too. Not just to fact check, but to live a deeper faith where we are interacting with the Word, instead of choking down a second-hand faith. Sometimes people are wrong. That doesn't mean that they are bad leaders or bad Christians. But we need to know why we believe what we think we believe, and where to find it for ourselves.

We all have opinions about things, but when you feel strongly about something—especially something that involves the Lord, his Word, or his people—it is important to make sure that your belief comes from the truth in God's Word. Our opinions should be God's opinions. This can show up in a couple different ways. We may have to adjust our thinking if God's Word is specific about a subject.

Sex outside of marriage is wrong. We see a good example of this in the woman caught in adultery. (Adultery is not just when a person is married and has sex with someone else. Adultery is having sex with anyone to whom you aren't married.) Jesus saves her from death and tells her to go and sin no more. (I know you know this passage; I've mentioned it before.) Sex feels good, and it seems like so many other people are doing it and justifying it. But if Jesus said, "Go and sin no more," that means that we need to give up our selfishness and live differently. Our opinions need to be God's opinions, even if it isn't easy or convenient. Even if it involves sacrifice and not fitting in all the time.

I'm not saying that we should be people full of doubt and mistrust, but I think we should be so firmly rooted in Scripture that we are finding our truth from the Lord, and not solely from the thoughts of others. God is okay with our questions. That's why he gave us a book of answers. We just need to be committed to using it, instead of being satisfied with a lazy faith that rides on the backs of others and hopes for the best.

Questions for Reflection:

- Describe your conversion experience. How did you first meet Jesus? If you can't remember, or if you haven't yet, do you want to make Jesus a part of your life today? Find a friend or leader and pray the prayer of salvation with him or her. Then celebrate!
- Are there any areas of your faith that you aren't sure about? Maybe there are things you've learned that you question? Do some research on those areas today, and try to answer your questions using God's Word and trusted sources.
- Search your heart to be sure that your opinions are God's opinions, and they are not just based on what you may have heard from others, or on things that make you feel comfortable and justified.
- What are some tough Scriptures that you may need to wrestle with?

Season of Terror

The word "terror" is used often in our world, and never in reference to anything good. We talk about terrorists being a threat to national security. We talk about domestic terrorism, when Americans use destructive force to incite fear and panic. We even use the word terror when describing kids who face extreme harassment in school or online. These are examples of terror that involve others. But there is a different type of terror I want to talk about in this chapter. That is the terror that comes from losing your faith.

I hope you can see the connection, because they can often feel very similar. Picture in your mind the news footage from a bombing or attack. My most recent memories are of the Boston marathon bombing. When this happened, it sent our nation reeling. Who did this? Why? When will we catch them? Will the injured be okay? I still picture smoke and debris all over. People lying on the ground or scattering in every direction. Chaos. What comes next? When will we feel normal again?

By nature, I am a doubter. I struggle with faithlessness and doubt more than anything else. Some people are crippled by sin or a behavior that they just can't seem to stay away from. That's not my story. Yeah, I sin and fall short, but the thing that keeps setting me back in my journey with the Lord isn't a tangible sin, it's my lack of faith.

This is something that I need to keep in the forefront of my thinking. The doubting thoughts rise up quietly at first. I will think things like, *That Scripture they just read seems ridiculous. That can't be true.* Sometimes when the dark cloud of doubt starts to swallow me up, I recognize it for what it is—doubt, not truth—and I run to the feet of Jesus in prayer. I surround myself with people I can be honest with and they keep me accountable while still showing me grace. Then there are times when I feed those thoughts, and I quickly find myself in a dark place of disbelief and mistrust. My internal life feels very much like the scene from the Boston bombing. I am lost and can't see through the smoke and shrapnel.

That is when I feel the terror. My whole identity is Jesus. When I lose my faith, who am I? This is a disturbing experience for any Christian. But I think this is even more terrifying when you are a professional Christian. That's what pastors really are, isn't it? It's my job to be the best Jesus follower I can be, and to teach others to do the same. Jesus is my motivation to do everything I do. I feed the hungry for Jesus. Teach kids in the hood that life can be different because of Jesus. Who am I and what do I do if I don't buy any of it?

This would be like a professional artist losing the ability to see. How would the artist paint? Would the artist have to find a new identity? What would come next? Would there be any way for the artist to regain the ability to see? That would be terrifying.

Because this is my struggle, it happens every few years. The blackness of terror swallows me up and traps me with my own fear and doubt. The longer I walk with Jesus, the greater the time between these personal terror attacks. But I was in the middle of the worst one during the summer of 2014. We were gearing up to start our fourth summer running camp, and I felt desperately alone and separate from God. I vacillated between not knowing who God was right then, and the fear that someone would find out and my façade would be ripped away.

Camp started and things were going well, really well. Our staff was on point, and I could see God moving all around. You would think that would reignite the spark in me, but it just made me feel more desperate, and that desperation sometimes led to anger. There were times I woke up that summer and thought, *I don't think I believe in God today.* That isn't something I would wish on my worst enemy.

We had discipleship groups for our staff after the worship services. I led one of those groups during this time. I had an amazing group of ladies who were a true blessing in my life. One of those ladies was Antoinette, but everyone calls her Nettie. (This is really good, because Antoinette is kinda hard to pronounce. This is also her real name.)

After the second week at camp, I decided that I was going to do all I could to climb out of this pit of darkness. Part of that was being honest about how I was feeling, and how much I wanted to reconnect with Jesus. This is much easier to say than it is to do, especially for leaders. We need to walk the tightrope of being honest, but not too honest. Be vulnerable, but don't share all your dirties. Let people see you for who you are, but make sure that your really personal stuff stays personal. I think this is a farce. Either you let people see you for who you are, or you don't. Yeah, we gotta gauge what is appropriate, but if you are intentionally holding back to maintain an image you think you need to keep up, you are lying.

Back to discipleship group. We are in there, sitting in a circle on the floor of the chapel (it sounds very kum ba yah, but it really wasn't) and I started to share that I felt really distant from the Lord and I didn't know what to do to get back, if it was even possible. I cried, and as I shared I felt a sliver of hope make its way into my darkness. I knew I had people praying for me, and even if I wasn't any closer to Jesus yet, knowing that it wasn't a secret was a relief in itself.

We kept meeting, week after week, until the summer was almost over. We met for discipleship and we all shared about how we were doing and how we could pray for each other. Things with me and Jesus were on the upswing. I didn't have any more of those mornings where I doubted the existence of God. But there were still times when I questioned some elements of my faith and felt distant from him. I shared about this, and when the group was over, Nettie took me aside.

Please keep in mind that Nettie was a counselor, new to our camp, and new in her relationship with me. I can be kind of intimidating being that I am big, and I was the boss. But Nettie cared enough about my soul to have a tough conversation with me. She said, "Mama Lisa (most of our staff called me this), you are doing so much for Jesus, and your tank is less than half full. Think of the amazing things you could do for the Lord if you were filled to the brim and fully connected." That is just what I needed to hear. I started to cry and Nettie asked if she could pray for me. I thankfully agreed. What happened next was something that I'd never experienced before.

Nettie put her hand on my shoulder and prayed a prayer that changed my life. She asked God to remove all the doubt and fear from my heart, that I would be able to see Jesus for who he really is and how much he loves me and wants to walk with me even when I can't see it. She asked for restoration and hope. She said a bunch of other stuff, but I can't remember it all because I was crying the whole time. Not just trickles of tears, but big drops that flowed continuously and messed up my makeup. My shoulders were shaking and my heart cracked open.

While she prayed I felt the power of the Holy Spirit moving and it was like I heard him say, "Lisa, I'm here. I see you. I know. I love you. Please let me in again."

And that was it.

The pit was gone and Jesus and I are closer than we've ever been. Maybe it's like when people in recovery talk about rock bottom. I've been to my spiritual rock bottom, and I will do everything I can to never experience that again.

Everything feels off balance when God is absent. My whole life was being sucked into the pit, and there is a good chance that things wouldn't have gotten better if I had kept it to myself. If you haven't ever known what this terror is like, I hope you never do. But you might. Life is hard. This dark night of the soul can happen to anyone. I would encourage you to be honest about this hurt if it sneaks its way into your life. Don't feel shame or work hard to keep up a front. Share the struggle with those you love, and climb out together.

In Matthew 17, we find a story about a boy who is possessed and this possession has led to seizures. The boy's dad brings the boy to the disciples so they can heal him. But for some reason the disciples are unable to make this boy right. Then the man brings his son to Jesus and tells him this. Jesus gets angry and tells the disciples that they are an unbelieving and perverse generation. Jesus is like, "How long am I gonna have to put up with you?" He heals the boy and once the boy and his dad are gone, the disciples ask why they couldn't heal the boy. *"Because you're not yet taking God seriously," said Jesus. "The simple truth is that if you had a mere kernel of faith, a poppy seed, say, you would tell this mountain, 'Move!' and it would move. There is nothing you wouldn't be able to tackle"* (Matt. 17:20 MSG).

The disciples walked and talked with Jesus every day, and they still had doubt.

I think Scripture includes several instances of the disciples' doubt to show us that it's normal, and when we doubt or have moments where our faith waivers, God is bigger than all of it. God gets it, and wants to see us through to the other side. Even if that faith is just a teeny, tiny mustard seed, it will grow and blossom if it is nurtured.

If you find yourself in this place of doubt and despair, what are you going to do about it? I got to my dark place because I listened to and fed the questions that separated me from Jesus. If I would have recognized that for what it was, and had a plan to conquer it, everything would have been different. So as you are in the place of darkness, make a plan to build a ladder to climb out. Maybe the rungs of that ladder will be friends you can be honest with. Integrate Scripture into more of your life. Pray to God even if you don't hear anything back at first. Plan to succeed. Plan to get better. Plan to reunite with Jesus. That's the best plan any of us could ever make.

Questions for Reflection:

- When have you experienced a time of doubt or faithlessness?
- Who are some people you can be honest about your faith with?
- Are there any conversations you need to have today on your journey toward a right relationship with Jesus?
- What are some Scriptures about doubt and restoring faith?

The Fight

"Can you hide me?"

I was twenty-one years old and seven months pregnant. I worked at a local jewelry store in Salinas, California, fixing watches. This was my least favorite job ever, even worse than working at Hot Dog on a Stick. No contact with people, lots of contact with small watch parts that I had to wear magnifying lenses on top of my glasses to see. (Good thing I was pregnant and married, otherwise I don't know how I would have kept the boys away.) Good job to have when you are pregnant, bad job to have when you are ... me.

It was a late afternoon at the end of fall when a petrified teenage girl burst through the doors of the jewelry store. Let's call her Janet. She was so skinny I was surprised she had the strength to push the door open. I would estimate her to have a similar waist circumference to that of my thigh (my normal big girl thigh, not my seven-month-pregnant thigh—that thigh was HUGE). Her hair was a hot mess, and she was clearly running from someone. When Janet came through the door, she made eye contact with me and asked, "Can you hide me?"

I was confused to say the least.

"From who?" This answer would determine the rest of the afternoon. If the answer had been the cops, then my response would have been, "No thanks, please try next door."

"From my pimp," she said as she walked to the counter. She had my attention. She told me that she had a ticket for a Greyhound bus, but needed a place to hide until it was time to board. Janet was going home, running away from the life that had her tangled up. She told me a little of what life had been like, and I knew that I was going to do all I could to make sure Janet got on that bus safely.

She sat at my feet, hidden behind the counter, until it was time to leave. I texted my husband this short message while we waited: "A teen prostitute just came into shop. She needs my help. Please pray. I love you." He tried to call me, but it was time to go. I walked her to the door and she started to say thank you as if our time together were ending. I stopped her and said I wasn't going to leave until that bus drove away with her on it.

Janet looked at my giant pregnant belly and told me that it wasn't safe. There was a good chance that her pimp was in the area surrounding the bus station looking for her. He wouldn't be afraid to hurt me to get her back. At that point I had to make a decision. Which life had more value? Was my unborn baby worth more than Janet? If we really believe that every life has value, and that the Lord really loves everyone the same, then there is only one answer. Janet's life was just as important as that of my baby.

Together we walked the few blocks to the bus stop. Janet was shaking in fear the whole way. I reached over and grabbed her hand and held it as we walked. I wanted to help her. I wanted to comfort and nurture her. I wanted to share the saving grace of Jesus with her. But all I could do was hold her hand. Sometimes just being there with others when they are in the middle of a storm is enough.

A weight lifted as we walked through the doors of the bus station and saw the security guards. I could tell Janet felt a little safer. We looked at the board above our heads that told us when her bus was leaving. It had been delayed and was now almost an hour behind schedule. She started sobbing and said, "He'll find me by then for sure."

I grabbed Janet by both bony shoulders, my belly touching her sunken ribs, and said, "I told you I was going to stay with you the whole time. You will be safe. You will go home." I hoped that she believed me. I hoped that I believed me.

We found a set of seats together in a corner. I sat next to her, trying to block people's view of her the best I could. I pictured her pimp exploding through the doors, determined to regain his human property. Then I imagined standing up and fighting back with the force and agility of an action movie star, while trying to lean my belly out of the way. None of this happened (thankfully). We sat together, not speaking, just holding hands until it was time. Looking back, people around us probably thought we were a couple, but were probably very confused by both of our conditions.

Janet waved as her bus drove away.

I stood with Janet in the middle of her fear and uncertainty because Jesus did it for me. He does it for me every day. Being Jesus to the lost and hurting often involves extreme courage. Doing things for the cause of Christ doesn't always seem sane, or safe, or comfortable. We express courage in times of distress in our lives or in others' lives because we know that we have already won. Jesus paid the price for us. If our end game is living Jesus and loving others, then we jump in and stand up for what's right, even if it is scary, even if it may lead to the unknown.

Most of the time standing up for justice and doing what is right will not lead to a life-threatening situation. But even if it does, would you stand up for the oppressed or those being hurt? Would you be willing to live out your faith at all costs, or are you an evangellyfish—someone who expresses your faith when it feels comfortable and when the situation isn't threatening? Is the backbone of who you are in Christ firm and strong no matter what, or is it so bendable that when things get hard your passion for Jesus becomes invisible?

"Do not be afraid of those who kill the body but cannot kill the soul. Rather, be afraid of the One who can destroy both soul and body in hell. Are not two sparrows sold for a penny? Yet not one of them will fall to the ground outside your Father's care. And even the very hairs of your head are all numbered. So don't be afraid; you are worth more than many sparrows" (Matt. 10:28-31 NIV).

This is an extreme verse to go with an extreme example. It is not often here in America that we do things as a reflection of our faith that put our physical lives into danger. But there are things we can do as people of justice that will put our comfort to death, or our reputations to death, or even end some important relationships.

We need to be people of strong backbones. People of courage, willing to really act for Jesus instead of wanting to change the world, but instead spending all of our time talking about it while we sip our overpriced coffee and sit behind our computer screens, "liking" all the latest social justice trends, while in reality, we are doing absolutely nothing about it.

It's time to get off our butts! What are you doing today to impact injustice? Do you step over the same homeless person every day without ever asking his name or offering him something to eat? Do you know of things in our world that grieve the Holy Spirit, but you choose to ignore them or wait for someone else to fix them? It's our turn to fight injustice with our faith and courage, knowing that Jesus is who he says he is, and is empowering us to do the things he would do.

How are you going to change the world?

People might make fun of you. Some might tell you that it's too big, or that you are too small. People you love may get jealous or angry and try to make you stop. Are you ready for criticism that doesn't come from love and kindness? Are you courageous? We don't have to have all the answers right away; we just have to be brave and willing.

I wish I could tell you that Janet got home and was fully embraced by her family. I wish I could say that she totally left the old life behind and found freedom in Christ and in a new identity. Truth is, I don't know what happened to Janet after that bus rolled out of sight.

When we do things to make a difference, we aren't always guaranteed a perfect outcome. Sometimes you may not even know what the outcome is. But as Christians, as soldiers, we live by the courageous truth of Jesus and the motto of fighting to the end.

William Booth gave these words in a famous address: "While women weep, as they do now, I'll fight; while children go hungry, as they do now, I'll fight; while men go to prison, in and out, in and out, as they do now, I'll fight; while there is a poor lost girl upon the streets, while there remains one dark soul without the light of God, I'll fight, I'll fight to the very end!"

Fighting demands courage. Fighting demands action. Fighting isn't comfortable or safe, and it doesn't even offer a sure outcome. Will you commit to fighting injustice today?

Questions for Reflection:

- What needs do you see in your community that you could start affecting?
- What are practical things you need to do this?
- Who is going to be on the team that fights and serves and loves in this cause?
- What will you do if people don't believe in your fight, or make fun of it?
- What are some Scriptures that talk about this kind of action?

The Curse of Coasting on Good Enough

In high school I was a horrible student. The second half of my freshman year, I earned an "F" or "Incomplete" in all of my classes. Things got slightly better from that point on, but I adopted the motto "D's earn degrees" to justify not having to do well to move forward.

It was because of my lack of drive to succeed that I spent five years in high school. If you aren't aware, this is also known as being a "super senior." I didn't feel super. I felt like a big dummy who couldn't get it together. I didn't do the bare minimum to get by, but even if I did do just enough, that still isn't success. That's just ... good enough.

When I think of the things people might say about me when I'm not around, one of the worst insults would be, "Oh Lisa, yeah I think I know who she is. She is that chick who's alright. She's good enough." Talk about apathy! If others define you as "good enough," you are so lackluster they don't even have an opinion of you. It reminds me of Emmet in The Lego Movie. The other characters in the movie all kinda know who he is, but there isn't anything special that sticks out in their minds, because Emmet only follows the instructions and gets lost in the crowd. I would feel better if someone said, "Oh Lisa, that chick is nuts! She does crazy things." At least then I would be seen as someone who does something. Not everyone is going to agree with me all of the time, but clashing with people over my ideas is far better than not even bringing anything to the table for them to disagree with.

I don't want to be a placeholder. I don't want to be a person who just takes up space. I don't want to be mediocre and I don't want to be just good enough.

Once I walked into a job that was a hot mess, one I wasn't prepared for, and at the time I didn't even want. All the while I was surrounded by people waiting for me to fail, and letting me know it at every opportunity.

The song of the crowd changed quickly, and I wish I could say that it was because I stepped on the stage and went above and beyond in every aspect of my ministry. I wish it was because I was a visionary leader and a phenomenal speaker. I wish people changed their opinion of me because of my skill set or my Mother Theresa-like service and kindness. But really, I just showed up and did the bare minimum.

There were so many festering wounds in the relationships that surrounded this ministry that even just being mediocre, it seemed like I was doing great things. I coasted on good enough for almost two years. TWO YEARS. That's a long time to be content in being average.

I was only doing average work not because I was lazy, but because I was sad. I missed my old home and friends. Ministry became something I never thought it would, and I turned inward. I focused on myself instead of others, and I lost sight of what mattered most.

I wasted two years of God's time caught up in a bad attitude, and full of selfishness. Mediocre had become my standard. This is a crappy place to live, but there could be worse things. There had been worse things. But just because mediocrity isn't a huge noticeable or tangible sin doesn't mean that it's not a destructive behavior that sets us back from who God created us to be.

There are people who are so competitive that they will do anything to be in first place. They have to be the very best at everything. Please don't hear me say that this is a better place to be, because it's just not. Living a life fighting to be number one gets lonely, quick. That way of operating pushes people out of the way as you run to reach the finish line first. I want to be—and be with—people who succeed and do great things, but not at the expense of others, either in action or in comparison.

Being THE BEST shouldn't be our goal. Instead our aim should be to be our best, as people who work hard for an end game that we care about. We don't have to win the race every time, but we should at least be attempting to beat our own previous record.

I like to hike. (This isn't sarcasm; I really do enjoy hiking.) Living in Arizona, hiking sometimes also means light mountain climbing. There is this great spot a few miles away from my house called Camelback Mountain. One day my son and I woke up so early the sun wasn't up yet. We drove to the base of this mountain and started making our way to the top, with plenty of chubby kid breaks along the way. I made sure to pack plenty of water and good snacks. (Sometimes I go hiking just for the trail mix.) We got about halfway up the mountain, which is something to be proud of, especially when you are a thirty-year-old sedentary mother of two and a nine-year-old boy.

A few months later we decided to try it again, this time from a different entry point to the mountain. This starting point led to a much more challenging trail than the first time. We spent most of the time talking about how amazing the view was going to be when we got to the very top. After almost an hour and a half, we were only three quarters of the way up, and were exhausted out of our minds. The terrain had changed from a smooth dirt trail to pebbles that were just a bit larger than sand, and our feet were slipping with every step.

We stopped for a water break (and maybe a snack—don't judge me). I tried to push Little Ant to go further. The summit was so close, I could see it. Ant, in all his young wisdom, looked at me and said, "Mom, this is so much further than we went last time. This is our personal best!" He had done better than the time before, and was justifiably proud of himself. We called it finished, pretended to stick a flag in the ground, man-on-the-moon style, and started down the mountain.

We didn't have to get to the very top to do well. My boy was totally gassed out. He really gave all he had to get to that point on the mountain. If we had done the hike just like we had before, stopped where we did the last time, we wouldn't have known how great it feels to give all we had, or the gratification that came from surpassing the standard that we had previously set.

So many of us coast on good enough at work or school, in ministry or relationships. But mediocre effort produces mediocre results, and mediocre results lead to mediocre lives.

Life can be so much better than good enough. Yeah, pushing yourself comes with more possible failure. But it also brings more possible success, and more encouragement, and more quality change for the kingdom.

Some of us come from families of good enoughs, others from families who are content with even less. If this is you, then you have probably been rewarded and praised in mediocrity. God doesn't expect you to be perfect, or better than anyone else (I don't even think God operates in those terms). But God created you and he knows you and what you are capable of. He wants the best for you, even if no one else is pushing you to succeed. God made you for great things, not just good enough things.

In light of all this, here's what I want you to do. While I'm locked up here, a prisoner for the Master, I want you to get out there and walk—better yet, run!—on the road God called you to travel. I don't want any of you sitting around on your hands. I don't want anyone strolling off, down some path that goes nowhere. And mark that you do this with humility and discipline—not in fits and starts, but steadily, pouring yourselves out for each other in acts of love, alert at noticing differences and quick at mending fences (Eph. 4:1-3 MSG).

We work hard and give our best, not so that we can be the best but because we serve the best. Coasting on good enough as a follower of Jesus will never be good enough. There are too many things to get done, too many people who are hurting, too many without clean water or shelter, too many who are trapped in homelessness or hunger, too many who are living in despair because they haven't heard the life-changing truth of Jesus. They deserve our best—not for me to strive to be better than you, but for you to strive to be better than you.

In the Scripture we see that God wants us to work hard and be successful in different areas, including noticing our differences and quickly mending fences. God wants us to be people of discipline in our actions, who are attentive in our relationships with others, too. He wants us to be people who say, "Come along with me as we succeed together," as opposed to, "Get out of the way. You just aren't good enough, and I have things to do." Achieving our goals and surpassing the standard expectations are important, but never as important as the love we show as we serve him and others.

The harder we work to achieve great things, the more opportunities people have to say, "Look at the great things God is doing in their lives!" They realize that if God can remove us from the grip of good enough, he surely can do it for them, too.

Questions for Reflection:

- Have there been areas in your life where you didn't strive to do your best because you knew that meeting the bare minimum would be good enough?
- How are you going to live differently today to break free from the curse of coasting on "good enough"?
- What are some Scriptures that talk about the value of working hard and giving your best?
- Are there any people you need to apologize to for giving a shallow effort?

Exploding Pedestals

People fall from grace all the time. Sometimes our favorite authors are revealed as plagiarists. Sometimes the musicians we connect with steal ideas from others. Couples whose marriages we respect get divorced. Spiritual leaders we admire have major moral failures. Christians we strive to be like, fall short and let us down.

Sometimes people suck. Even the ones we put on a pedestal. Even the ones who seem like they have it all together. People will let us down, even the ones we admire the most. That is probably when we are most affected by the humanness of others, when the ones who seem infallible show us they are capable of failure just like we are.

I was twenty-two years old when I walked in the door of my seminary. I was young and naive about a great many things. In my mind, the people who would surround me for the next two years were going to be the best of the best. These were people who had just given up their whole lives to devote themselves to the study of God's Word in preparation for becoming pastors and officers in The Salvation Army. These people would exude kindness and compassion. These people would all be amazing, selfless leaders who listened and loved unabashedly, no matter what was going on in their own lives. I was looking forward to watching them live like this, because that's who I wanted to be, but totally was not. They were going to show me how to be a pastor in training, because I was clueless but sure that they would have it figured out.

The other half of the people who would surround me would be people who had already arrived. These were folks who were seasoned leaders and teachers. People who were experienced and educated and knew all the answers to anything I would ever ask. I was sure these people would all be calm and even zen-like in their reactions and responses to all life threw their way. That's how spiritual dudes are supposed to be, right? I had no idea, but I went into this place of theological and practical education with the highest possible expectations.

For the first few weeks, things seemed to be relatively on track with what I expected. Then it happened. They showed me their humanity. How could they make mistakes like this? Didn't they know I had put them all on unrealistic pedestals that no one could ever attain? They were supposed to have it all together! I was so disappointed.

I hope you can hear how ridiculous my expectations were. I really thought those things. I set people up on platforms they didn't ask for, with unfair and unrealistic responsibilities. I know that now, as future Lisa looks back on past Lisa. But I didn't see these expectations as unrealistic at the time, and when people let me down, it threw me for a loop.

I think everything would have been different if I would have known that people, even the cool ones that we admire and respect, are bathed in sin and weakness and failure—just like me, and just like you. We all have demons knocking at our door and temptations we have to deny. None of us are perfect, and none of us are infallible. And it's not fair to expect that from anyone.

When I first realized that even the mighty fall, it caused some doubt and more questions than I had answers. I thought, *If they can't make it through without falling on their faces, what makes me think I can? If they fall short, there is no way I will be able to achieve anything.* I questioned everyone, and became suspicious of everything. How could any of this be attainable if they couldn't get it right? I mean, I knew that I couldn't get it right—but they seemed so much better than me. I lost hope.

I think this type of reaction from me was an example of my baby faith. I wasn't mature in the Word, and I didn't really know what it was like to have a deep relationship with God that was rooted in my connection with Jesus. For me, my relationship with God was often experienced through my relationships with other people. I thought things like, *I don't know how to serve selflessly, but Jen does, so let me watch her to figure it out,* when really I should have been thinking, *I don't know how to serve selflessly, so let me spend time in prayer, searching the Scriptures to figure it out.*

When we put our hope and faith in people instead of the Messiah, we will always be disappointed, even if we choose to idolize the people who seem like they really get it right. People will make mistakes. People will cause hurt or disappointments. People are people, and in our humanness we will fall short. Praise God for the example and gift of Jesus! That dude had it right. That is the dude we emulate and strive to be like. Jesus was and will always be perfect. He will never hurt us or let us down.

He sits on the only pedestal that we should ever have, and it's not even a pedestal that is high or lofty. Jesus' pedestal can be found kneeling at the feet of a junkie, telling her that life can be better. Jesus' place of recognition and esteem is in cradling a child who feels unloved or abandoned. That's his example, that's what he does, and that's what he wants from us: to love and serve the least of these.

If there were ever people who we could justify living our faith vicariously through, they would be the people we read about in Scripture. These are individuals who literally walked and talked with Jesus, or knew God in an intimate way. They learned from the Master, and had the opportunity to see him in action. If it makes sense to have any humans on a pedestal, it would be the disciples and those who walked with the Lord.

But those guys were human, too.

Jacob was a hairless liar. Joseph was abused by his family. Moses had a speech impediment. Gideon was a chicken. Rahab sold her body. Timothy was a kid. David had an affair. Isaiah preached naked. Job went bankrupt. Jonah ran away from God. The Samaritan woman was living with her boyfriend. Judas betrayed Jesus. Thomas doubted. Peter denied Jesus. Martha freaked out about everything. John the Baptist ate bugs. They all fell asleep when they shoulda been praying or paying attention. Paul was too religious. Lazarus was dead.

Even these people had faults and made mistakes. When I was a baby in my faith, this realization brought feelings of defeat. But now, as I grow closer to God, these examples restore my hope that God can use anyone for his glory.

We don't have to live through the faith or example of others who will disappoint and let us down. Instead we live through the example of Jesus, knowing that if God used any of these fallen people to spread his truth, he could use us for sure. We aren't perfect, but God doesn't seem to be in the business of using perfect people (probably because he can't find any), just regular folks who are doing the best they can with what they have and wanting to give hope through it all.

Philippians 4:13 is a familiar verse: *For I can do everything through Christ, who gives me strength* (NLT). It doesn't say I can do anything through my leaders and role models and those who have it together or make all the right choices. It says we can do anything through Christ. Christ. Christ alone is our source of strength and hope. He is our example and our motivation.

When people fall short and let you down, know that God never will. He has things for you to do, great things that will change the world. He knows who you are and the hurts that have shaped your heart. He knows your fears and doubt and sees your wounds, even the ones you think you hide well. He sees the people you need to forgive, and the things you need to forgive yourself for. He sees your ability to make beautiful things and flap your creative wings. He knows where you have been unfairly judged or belittled and wants to heal those dark places of doubt and faithlessness. God knows the desires you have to love and serve the lost, even if you are afraid or not sure where to start. He is aware of your desire to be truly loved and to love others.

God is mindful of who you are, all you've ever been, and all you desire to be.

He believes in you even if you think no one does. He created you for wholeness and greatness. Today is your day to sing, to soar, and to serve with the confidence that you are made in the image of the creator of the universe and he has your back—today and forever. No matter what.

Questions for Reflection:

- Who have you held in the light of unfair expectations?
- Are there people you need to apologize to for your lack of grace?
- Is your faith rooted in Jesus, or in others?
- What are some Scriptures about following Jesus above all?

Conclusion

I'm not a writer. I'm just a person with a story to tell. A story about grace and redemption for a girl the world had told was unlovable and disposable. A story about unending, immeasurable compassion from a Savior who died for us when we were lost or in the gutter. A story about restoration and hope.

I was a whore's daughter, lost, afraid, and abandoned. Now I am a daughter of the King, redeemed, restored, and renewed by the grace of Jesus. My hope is that, through reading this book, you are able to see life and faith in a different light. It can be messy, but there is nothing more gratifying than walking this world with Jesus by your side.

I am thankful for those who've believed in me, even when I didn't believe in myself. I am thankful for my friends, who have taken up the place of family in my life. And I am most thankful for my husband, who has figured out how to balance loving me for me while encouraging me to grow and change into the person God desires me to be.

My favorite verse in all of Scripture is: *Not only that, but we rejoice in our sufferings, knowing that suffering produces endurance, and endurance produces character, and character produces hope* (Rom. 5:3-4 ESV). This verse defines my life and my faith. No matter what comes my way, I will keep my eyes on Jesus and the hope that he brings, in spite of the troubles of this world.

He is faithful. He is love. He is our grace and redemption.

Photo by Ruben Cordero

About the author

Lisa Barnes is friggin crazy about Jesus. Born in Vegas, a product of a one night stand to a mother who was a prostitute and addict, Lisa uses her story and struggles as her lens through which she sees the world and her faith, and also as a spring board to love and serve anyone in her sphere of influence.

Lisa is passionate about social justice, loving those in the margins, fully being herself, while living and sharing Jesus. In her opinion those things are non-negotiable, most other things are debatable. She has ministered in Portland, Oregon, San Francisco, and Salinas, California. Lisa currently lives in Phoenix, Arizona as a Salvation Army officer (ordained minister) in charge of all things youth and young adult for her region. She holds a bachelor's degree in Counseling for Christian Ministries. Lisa loves art; both in creating it and enjoy others' creations. She's been married to her handsome best friend for eleven years. They live life with their two beautiful beige babies and their six year old fat cat.